G000162496

The Chelsea Centre Theatre Company presents
the world premiere of

Room to Let

by Paul Tucker

First performance at
the Chelsea Centre Theatre
6 May 1999

The Chelsea Centre Theatre Company presents
the world premiere of

Room to Let

by Paul Tucker

Cast (in order of appearance)

Roger	Grahame Fox
Eddie	Peter Hamilton
Janet	Karen E Jones

Production Team

Director	Sarah Frankcom
Designer	Ruth Paton
Assistant Designer	Janie Abbott
Dramaturg	Mel Kenyon
Lighting Designer	John Treherne
Sound Designer	Francis Watson
Casting	Amanda Frend
Stage Manager	Caroline Batt
Production Manager	John Treherne
Photography	David Micklem

GRAHAME FOX

Theatre includes: **The Last Yellow** (by Paul Tucker), Chelsea Centre; **Unlucky for Some** (by Paul Tucker), Southwark Playhouse.
Television includes: **The Knock** (Carlton); **The New Adventures of Robin Hood** (Warner Bros TV); **A Respectable Trade** (BBC); **The Bill** (Thames); **The Turnaround** (Carlton); **999** (BBC).
Film includes: **Bodywork** (Automatic Pilot Films); **O Mary This London** (BBC Films); **Bone Zero** (Modus Operandi Films); **Darklands** (Metrodome).

PETER HAMILTON

Theatre includes: **Absurd Person Singular; Absent Friends**, Edinburgh Festival; **Rufian on the Stair**, TPT; **The Cherry Orchard**, DoC; **The Party Card**, New End; **Early Hours of a Reviled Man**, Finborough; **Mathilda Lear**, Snarling Beasties; **Up 'n' Under**, Belgrade.
Television includes: **The Black Bag, Bute Town Boys; Mr Peach; Father of the Man**, (Channel Four).
Writing includes; **Switchboard**.

KAREN E JONES

Theatre includes: **North Pole** (winner of Guardian International Student Drama Award); **The Nun**, Battersea Arts Centre; **The Egg and Sperm Race**, The Bird's Nest; **Unlucky for Some** (by Paul Tucker), Southwark Playhouse; **Brighton Beach Scumbags**, Brockley Jack.

PAUL TUCKER

Theatre includes: **Happy Days are Here Again**, Royal Court Theatre Upstairs; **Unlucky for Some**, Leicester Haymarket; **The Last Yellow**, Chelsea Centre and tour.
Film includes: **A Great Day for Making Out** (Channel Four); **Final Moments** (Carlton TV, nominated as best Teleplay 1995 by the Writers' Guild of Great Britain); **The Last Yellow** (Jolyon Symonds Productions).

SARAH FRANKCOM

Theatre includes: **The Crows**, Royal National Theatre Studio; **Fear and Misery of the Third Reich**, Central School of Speech and Drama; **Creamy**, The Red Room; **Showstopper**, Edinburgh and the Arts

Theatre; **Undeveloped Land,**
Royal National Theatre
Studio / Chelsea Centre;
Confetti, Oval House /
Chelsea Centre.
Sarah is the Literary
Manager at the Royal
Exchange Theatre,
Manchester.

RUTH PATON
Theatre includes: **Odes and
Gameshows,** Camden
Peoples' Theatre; **Lady
Windermere's Fan,** Cockpit
Theatre; **Where the Heart Is,**
Pegasus Theatre, Oxford; **Six
Characters in Search of an
Author,** BADA; **The Lady's
Not for Burning,** Lyric Studio;
Ten by Pinter, Two's
Company; **Gamblers and
Crow,** BAC; **The Continuity
Man,** Sliced Eye Production
Company.

FRANCIS WATSON
Sound design includes:
Rhinoceros, Man in the
Moon; **Fossil Woman,** Lyric
Studio; **Pippin,**
Theatremanufaktur, Berlin;
The Little Prince, Young Vic
Studio; **Candide, Danton's
Death** and **Woyzeck,** all Gate
Theatre.
Direction includes: **Twelfth
Night,** HarlekinArt Festival,

Metz; **Les Femmes Savantes,**
Rose Bruford College.

JOHN TREHERNE
John is the Chelsea Centre's
Technical Manager.

The Chelsea Centre
Real people, real issues, real theatre

The Chelsea Centre develops and presents
new plays of high literary value dealing with
the issues of today. It is committed to
developing new audiences particularly those not usually well
served by theatre. Over the last eighteen months the Chelsea
Centre has presented world premieres of a number of new
plays including:

De Profundis by Merlin Holland
Firestarting by Julie Everton
Just, Not Fair by Jim Robinson
The Last Bus from Bradford by Tim Fountain
Ultraviolet by Jess Walters
Skinned by Abi Morgan
By Many Wounds by Zinnie Harris

In this period, the Chelsea Centre has seen two of its plays
(both co-productions with Moving Theatre) transfer to the
Royal National Theatre and to the Alley Theatre in Houston.
One of its premieres has been made into a full length feature
film and the Centre has received a prestigious Arts for Everyone
Award for its **Write Now** programme. This has enabled the
Centre to commission eight new writers whose work will be
presented at the Chelsea Centre over the next three years.

For the Chelsea Centre

Artistic Director	Francis Alexander
General Manager	David Micklem
Literary and Marketing Assistant	Kelly Maglia
Dramaturgical Consultant	Mel Kenyon
Education Manager	Lisa Mead
Technical Manager	John Treherne

The Chelsea Centre refurbishment project
Project Architect: Patrick Dillon Architect

In April 1998 the Chelsea Centre was awarded an Arts Council of England lottery grant to develop its plans for the refurbishment of its building. With accessibility at their core, the Centre's dynamic proposals will dramatically enhance the Centre's profile, creating a bright, airy and welcoming space for new and existing audiences. The comfort and accessibility of the building for our audiences and our performers will be reflected in a new café, increased gallery space, improved auditorium seating, accessible dressing rooms and enhanced sound and lighting facilities.

It is hoped that with further lottery funds the Chelsea Centre will be completely refurbished during the first half of next year with the building re-opening in autumn 2000.

If you are keen to find out more about the Chelsea Centre's refurbishment proposals please call David Micklem on 0171 352 1967.

The Chelsea Centre Limited Board of Directors: Tim Boulton, Merrick Cockell (Chairman), Michael Constantinidi, Adrian FitzGerald, Lady Hopkins, Nigel Mullan, Eva Rausing, Janet Suzman.

The Chelsea Centre Limited is a registered charity number 1060460.

Photo simulation: Patrick Dillon Architect

SUPPORTED BY
THE NATIONAL LOTTERY
THROUGH
THE **ARTS COUNCIL**
OF ENGLAND

Forthcoming new work

7 - 26 June at 8pm

The Chelsea Centre presents
the world premiere of
HAPPENSTANCE by Pete Lawson

Pete Lawson's latest play is both an epic journey across the
wilds of Northern Siberia and a return to the place of our birth.
Set partially in the huge new Chelsea and Westminster hospital
Happenstance is a poetic and visionary tale of love and death
that burns across our imaginations like a comet.

12 - 31 July at 8pm

The Chelsea Centre in association with Moving Theatre
presents the world premiere of
HOME BODY/KABUL by Tony Kushner

This is the story of a woman and a city. Or perhaps a love affair
or obsession with a country...

From the multi-award winning writer of **Angels in America**, this
is classic Kushner - provocative, funny, touching, inspirational.

Both plays now booking on 0171 352 1967.

The Chelsea Centre is a member of ITC

For Katja

First published in 1999 by Oberon Books Ltd.
(incorporating Absolute Classics)
521 Caledonian Road, London N7 9RH
Tel: 0171 607 3637 / Fax: 0171 607 3629

e-mail: oberon.books@btinternet.com

Copyright © Paul Tucker 1999

Paul Tucker is hereby identified as author of this work in accordance with section 77 of the Copyright, Designs and Patents Act 1988. The author has asserted his moral rights.

All rights whatsoever in this play are strictly reserved and application for performance etc. should be made before rehearsal to Casarotto Ramsay Ltd, National House, 60-66 Wardour Street, London, W1V 3HP. No performance may be given unless a licence has been obtained, and no alterations may be made in the title or the text of the play without the author's prior written consent.

This book is sold subject to the condition that it shall not by way of trade or otherwise be circulated without the publisher's consent in any form of binding or cover other than that in which it is published and without a similar condition including this condition being imposed on any subsequent purchaser.

A catalogue record for this book is available from the British Library.

ISBN 1 84002 125 X

Cover design: Andrzej Klimowski

Typography: Richard Doust

Printed in Great Britain by MPG Books Ltd, Bodmin

ROOM TO LET

Gary,

I love you, I envy you,
You are my moon, my stars,
my sun, and my black hole.

All the besteth,
Always a pleasure, never a chore,

Paul —

(some cunt).

SCENE ONE

*Lights fade up with music to reveal the living room of
a terrace house. It hasn't been decorated in years. A funeral
urn, a hospital gown, a pair of well-worn slippers along
with other regalia is strewn over the table. Next to the
table, a man in his fifties sits tied up in a chair. He wears
a surgical neck collar that has gone slightly brown over
time and a pair of glasses that make his eyes look bigger
than they actually are. He witters with dread and panic,
trying to break free as a younger man in his thirties
brandishes a pair of large pliers. He is bald, has a swedish
porn star type moustache and wears large and nasty
brown-tinted glasses. He approaches the man in the chair.
The man in the chair begins to cry, shaking his head,
begging. As the music draws louder, the younger man
inserts the pliers slowly into the other's mouth and starts to
pull out a tooth. The man screams. It is not a particularly
warming sound, rather like a animal being slaughtered.
Using Newton's theory of opposing forces, he pushes his
victim's forehead with one hand whilst he pulls with the
other. The man's screams become more terrifying, and as his
tooth comes out of its socket, his scream crescendos with the
bright and up-tempo music.*

EDDIE: Eddie's me name, chief. I'm 53. Live with me
partner Janet, big gel, just a terrace house on Milligan
Road, been there since we started seeing each other, be
over twenty years now. It's not a bad place, you've got an
off-licence on the corner, barbers round the back, not
that I ever use it really cause I've lost most of me hair.
I've never really had hair. I mean, I must have had hair
once, yer know, in me teens, but no, all gone now, just

some tufts round the back, pal. I live a quiet life really, don't go work, got made redundant over seven years ago, I don't do anything really. I suppose some'd say I'm boring, but when you get to my age in life, there aint a lot to do. Nothing really happens around here anyway. It's a bit of a quiet and peaceful neighbourhood. Janet can be very dominant sometimes. I mean, I'm a bit of a soft touch with women, tend to boss me about a bit, especially Janet. I mean, I'm not the brightest of blokes, never have been, got kicked in the head by a horse some years ago, perhaps that's why I'm a bit thick, bit slow. Looking back now, I could see it in her nature when we first met, she used to start screaming at me in pubs and stuff, or when we went on our holidays, we had to look everywhere for Yorkshire pudding cause she didn't fancy anything else, always had it her way, chief. We met through Lonely Hearts in the local paper. I've only had one other relationship but that was donkey's years ago, it just didn't work out, then I met Janet. We're trying to get a lodger in at the mo cause the daft sod's got it in her head to save some money up to get married. I've told her, you have to be very careful these days, can't trust anybody, you could end up living with one of those psychopaths...

JANET: I'm Janet, I'm 48, live with me partner, Eddie, been living together now for 24 years. Twenty-four years too long if you ask me. Met through Lonely Hearts, and I must have been lonely to meet him. Idle bleeder, he don't wanna go work, don't wanna take me on holiday, don't wanna do nought for me. He drives me mad sometimes, he aint got any get up and go, lazy. I've been waiting all these years for him to take me up the aisle. I mean, it's a girl's dream to get a ring on her finger, isn't it? That's why we're getting a lodger in, so we can have some money to pay for the honeymoon and such – cause he won't go out and earn it. I have to go out and earn, just a cleaning job at the infirmary, mind. We put an ad in the Post Office window last week, but no bugger's come to look at the room. Even if they did, they'd take one look at him, and leave. It isn't that I don't love Eddie, I mean, you get used to someone after all these years, you live and breathe 'em. I'd say I love him but I'm not in love with him if you get me meaning. I have to boss him around sometimes to motivate him, he's got no get up and go in him. I feel more like his mother at times than his wife. I aint lying but if I went away for a week, I'd come back and the house would look like a pigsty. I should have known from the start on our first date. He never had any money then and he hasn't got any money now. I had to buy the rounds! I know these days, a couple share rounds and stuff but in those days, it wasn't done for the woman to buy everything! His suit was all scruffy, he had bits of car oil over his shirt. He's the same now as he was then...

ROGER: I'm Roger, I come from Swansea and I'm 33. I'm an electrician, but at the end of the day, I can do any job, painting, decorating. If there's anything that needs doing, I can do it, know what I'm saying? Self taught an all. See, there wasn't a father-figure in my house so I learnt to do everything myself – plumbing, wiring, you name it. I've been driving round the country for the last couple of months because I'm on an adventure, can't tell you the whys and wherefores but there's a person I'm looking for see. I've been everywhere, the wedth and breadth of the country looking for said person, been to Leeds, I've done all of Wales, been to Bristol, all round that area, Gloucester, seen Stonehenge when I was there too. Saw the Yorkshire Moors, the downs, saw Warwick Castle, even had time to go round Gulliver's Kingdom but I thought Chessington Adventure Park had more to offer.

I've got a Cortina – F reg, be about twenny years old, but it's still in good nick, I did an overhaul on it what? Last year? Did all the interior out, fur-lined seats, car stereo, twin speaker, new paint job, did 90 straight the other week, all the way from Newark to Nottingham, and that wasn't even with my foot all the way down on the gas! I aint joking! Now I'm here, I'll keep looking for this person till the day I die. It was a promise I made see. It's become an obsession now. Won't tell you who it is though, you might let the cat out the bag, game'll be over then. But when I do find him, well, when I do find him – well we'll see. But I think I'm on his tail. He's caused more tears than will ever be shed for him...

SCENE TWO

Two days earlier. A Friday afternoon. EDDIE watches TV in a vest and suit trousers. The flicker of the TV lights up the room and EDDIE's glasses. EDDIE enjoys the TV but he hears someone approaching and a key turning in the door. EDDIE quickly gets up and turns the TV off. He sits back down and positions himself in such a way that it appears he's been like that all day. Enter JANET. She stands at the entrance of the door in her hospital cleaner's uniform. She stares at EDDIE. Sweat has gathered under her armpits. She carries two bags of shopping. EDDIE just pretends to read the paper. JANET goes over to the TV and feels the back of the TV set. It is warm. She takes off her shoe, goes over to EDDIE and hits him with it. She knows how to use it. EDDIE absorbs the attack.

JANET: What 'ave I told yer about watching telly in the day? (*She stops hitting him and points.*) Shopping.

EDDIE takes the bags into the kitchen and starts to unpack. JANET watches him with her arms folded.

JANET: Put it in, don't throw it in.

EDDIE: Stop watching me then.

JANET: I have to watch yer, make sure you do a proper job.

He continues putting the food away. EDDIE holds up a packet of something.

JANET: Cupboard.

He puts it in the cupboard. He holds up something else.

JANET: Fridge... (*Something else.*) Fridge... Freezer.

He puts the shopping in the fridge. JANET changes her standing position so that she can see him put things in the fridge. He takes out a family bag of crisps.

EDDIE: Why do you always have to get these ones?

JANET: Why? What's up with 'em?

EDDIE: They're crap. They stick in yer throat.

JANET: They're good enough for you.

EDDIE: They always put too much salt in 'em.

JANET: Now listen here monkey-man, I buy you sodding good food so don't start arguing with me.

EDDIE: You have 'em then.

JANET: (*Proud.*) I shall have 'em. I shall have 'em on bread.

JANET takes off her coat and hangs it up. EDDIE finishes the unpacking and sits back down, picks up the paper so that he doesn't have to look at her or speak to her. JANET sits down on the sofa ready for her second attack.

JANET: I suppose you aint been out today either. (*EDDIE shakes head.*) It's a good job I go out int it, go out to work so we can get some money in. I sweat cobs for you.

EDDIE: (*Prodding himself with thumb.*) I spent 12 years in the hosiery industry missus, so don't go round telling me about going out.

JANET: Phhh! Twelve years! Twelve days more like.

EDDIE: I've told yer, I daren't go out cause someone keeps following me.

JANET: Follow yer! Who wants to follow you? The only thing that follows you, is yer own bad smell.

EDDIE: Listen pal, I know when someone's following me, alright?

JANET: Well you could do something for me then, do some house work. You needn't pull that face either – go out and get a job.

EDDIE: (*Tiresome.*) I... don't... want... a... job.

JANET: Yes you do! It aint right for a man to sit in the house all day.

EDDIE: It aint right for a man to work all day.

JANET: (*Tuts, shakes head in disgust.*) People have to go out to work to get money. So they can live, so they can afford holidays or go pickernicking in the country.

EDDIE: I don't wanna go on picnics.

JANET: Well I do! I wanna go out now and again! I've been stuck in this house for the last 24 years! (*Gets out Argos catalogue from handbag, puts it on table.*) I've bought that for yer as well.

EDDIE: What do I want that for?

JANET: So you can get me an engagement ring. (*Gets out Butlins holiday brochure.*) And I've got yer that so yer can take me on our honeymoon.

EDDIE: (*Pulls head back.*) Aww you aint still going on about bloody marriage are yer?

JANET: Listen, I've been waiting half my bloody life for a ring on this finger.

EDDIE: Look, what's the point in getting married when we've been living together all these bleeding years?

JANET: (*Shaking fist.*) Cause... it... shows... me... how... much... you... love... ME.

EDDIE: Aww Christ.

JANET: You don't wanna marry me do yer?

EDDIE: Aww God forbid me.

JANET: You don't love me do yer?

EDDIE: I do!

JANET: Well what yer scared of then? Have you got another wife or something?

EDDIE: No!

JANET: Well you can take me up that bloody aisle then. I aint waiting any longer. I want a July wedding. And then we're going to Butlins for our honeymoon. Are you listening?

EDDIE: (*Reading paper.*) Yeah.

JANET: Well you could show a bit more excitement then!

EDDIE: What?

JANET: Oh forget it, I mind's well talk to meself. Be a lot more interesting. God, if I knew my life would end up like this when I was a teenager, I would have drowned meself.

EDDIE: If I knew my life would end up like this, I would have done it for yer.

JANET: (*Nodding.*) I'll remember that when you wanna borrow some money.

EDDIE: Listen, listen to me luv. We haven't got no money to get married. It's sodding expensive these days.

JANET: That's why we're getting a lodger in! I keep telling yer! If we charge 30 quid a week for that room, we'll have saved more than enough in a couple of months. That reminds me, has anyone bin?

EDDIE: Look luv, let's just take one thing at a time. You can't be hasty with these things – we might end up with one of those axe murderers or something.

JANET: Aww shurrup yer daft sod. You're just scared of having a real man around. Yes you are! You're scared to see what real men are like instead of farting and belching round the house all day.

JANET kicks off her shoes. She rubs her feet. Sweat has come through the toe bits in her tights. She takes off her tights, holds them out to EDDIE.

JANET: Here, you can hang these up an all. Give 'em a good airing.

EDDIE sighs, gets up, hangs the american tan tights near the window. JANET takes the tub of margarine off the table, scoops some out and rubs marg into her feet. EDDIE resumes his paper-reading. She clearly enjoys rubbing in the marg, pursing her lips, giving out slow huffs and puffs and pulling faces of 'what a day'.

JANET: Aww me footsies ache they do. I've been on 'em all day. Joyce at work, her husband rubs her feet for her. She doesn't have to ask him to rub her toes. He rubs crême fraîche into 'em. You wunt do that for me!

EDDIE sighs, rolls his eyes back. As she starts on the other foot, she finds a piece of paper screwed up between the cushions. She unwraps it. EDDIE hides behind his newspaper. She reads it.

JANET: Oi! What the hell's this?

EDDIE: (*Playing dumb.*) What?

JANET: You know what! (*Reads it.*) "Came to look at room this afternoon... Knocking for ages... Could hear the racing on the television... but nobody came to the door... will return this evening... thank you kind sirs... bye... " How long 'as this been here?

EDDIE: Dunno what yer talking about.

JANET: (*Pushing bottom set of teeth out.*) How... LONG... has this been here?

EDDIE: I'm not sure.

JANET: HOW LONG?

EDDIE: Since today!

JANET: Well why dint you let the bleeder in and show him the room?

EDDIE: Cause I don't wanna get married and I don't want a bleeding lodger!

JANET quickly scoops off the excess marg off her foot and wipes it back into the tub. She storms over to EDDIE. EDDIE lifts his arm up to protect himself.

JANET: (*Grabs his ear.*) Listen here pally – we're getting a lodger and then you're taking me up the 'kin aisle!

BLACKOUT.

SCENE THREE

Later that evening. JANET is rushing around tidying the flat between putting make-up on in the mirror. She places three plates and a loaf of bread on the table with a bottle of tomato sauce. She spits on a tissue and wipes away dried sauce off the lid. She is excited. EDDIE combs what little hair he has left. He wears his best cardigan over his vest. He is not excited. The sound of a car can be heard pulling up outside the house followed by the sound of a novelty car horn. JANET rushes over to the window.

JANET: Quick. D'yer reckon it's him? Aww look at the nice car he's got.

EDDIE: (*Looks out of window.*) It's a Cortina, don't mean he's rich.

JANET: He must be rich. Look, he's got fur around the seats.

JANET gives her hair a last buff up in the mirror before she answers. There is a knock at the door.

JANET: And you keep yer mouth shut, I don't want you putting him off.

JANET opens the door to ROGER. He wears a feathery ginger-blond wig and wears a cheap second-hand sweater with is tucked into ill-fitting farah hopsack trousers which are short in length. He wears eighties winklepickers with white socks. All this is topped off with a Swansea FC tattoo

*on one forearm and 'Mother' on the other. Together with the
tinted glasses, the moustache and the above attire, he thinks
he's cool and trendy, the man about town.*

ROGER: A room to let?

JANET: That's right. Come in

ROGER: Bloody murder trying to find this place I tell yer,
but I'm here all the same.

JANET: (*Laughs.*) Better late than never.

ROGER: (*Points.*) That's right, yeah.

JANET: I'll do the introductions shall a? I'm Janet.

ROGER: (*Kisses her hand.*) A pleasure to meet yer, Jan.

JANET: (*Embarrassed.*) Thank you.

ROGER: (*Sees EDDIE.*) And this must be yer husband?

JANET: (*Excited.*) Not yet, we're getting married in the
summer! Aren't we, Eddie? Aren't we?

EDDIE nods solemnly.

ROGER: (*A look of disgust, then shakes EDDIE's hand*)
Congratulations, Eddie. Pleased to meet yer.

EDDIE: Pleased to meet you too, pal. (*Studies ROGER's
face.*) Have we met before? Down the Legion or
something?

ROGER: Not that I know of. (*Pause.*) Perhaps you're
thinking of someone else.

EDDIE: Yeah, that must be it.

JANET: Ignore him, the daft bugger thinks someone's
following him! Are you hungry, Roger?

ROGER: So so. So so. I had a ploughman's earlier, in one of those Hungry Chefs. Fucking expensive an all. (*Reckons up.*) Four, no, hold on, five ninety nine for a ploughman's and a soft roll.

JANET: That's daylight robbery. I wunt go in 'em.

ROGER: Well see, what it is, Jan, what they do is, is they stick these Hungry Chefs on stretches where there aint a service station for miles. So they know, they know that they've got drivers by their whatsits, so when you go into one, (*As if intelligent.*) you're forced to pay their prices, and they know you'll pay it an all. That's how they make their money.

JANET: I know, it's disgusting.

ROGER: (*Taps change in pocket.*) The Hungry Chef sharnt be getting my custom again.

JANET: I should think not, prices they charge. Shall I show you the room then?

ROGER: (*One finger on nose, points.*) Good idea!

ROGER follows JANET into the hallway. They go upstairs. They can be heard talking and making polite conversation as they do so. EDDIE stands at the window and studies ROGER's car. Then he shakes his head, dismissing his suspicions that he knows ROGER from somewhere. JANET and ROGER come back into the living room.

JANET: ... And this is the living room and dining area. That's the kitchen in there, it's got all amenities, all modern appliances. I mean, we've already had 39 people come to look at the room but we wanted you to have first choice. Haven't we? Haven't we, Eddie?

EDDIE nods, disinterested.

ROGER: Aww that's lovely of yer.

JANET: So what do you think then?

ROGER: It's just what I'm looking for. (*JANET is pleased.*)
Could be in me dreams this place. See that door there?
If God walked through it and asked me what sort of
room I was looking for, then I'd tell him this one.

JANET: Ahh really?

ROGER: 'Kin lovely, this.

JANET: (*Blushing.*) Well, I do like to keep the place looking
nice.

ROGER: And that you do. I mean, you ought to see the
places I've seen in my time. Places that would break all
kinds of Health and Safety laws, I aint joking! Nine out
of ten, the landlord e'd be a wog. One Pakistani chap
even put a farquois on my head just cause I complained
about the taps not working.

JANET: (*Tuts.*) Oh I say.

ROGER: I mean, if your toilet seat breaks or you accidentally lose all yer curtain rails, these wogs, they won't
come round and mend 'em, they won't. Leave you to it
they do. I mean, you're fucked to buggery. Some of these
rooms aren't fit for human habitation, not even animals
would want to live in 'em, not even pigeons, and they're
the dirtiest bird I know, Jan.

JANET: (*Tuts.*) 'Ts disgusting. Shall we settle for tea then?

ROGER: That's the best idea I've heard all day!

*They all go to sit down at the table. EDDIE goes to sit down
in his usual place but ROGER sits down instead. EDDIE*

23

looks a bit put out, he takes another seat. ROGER rubs his hands together excitedly.

ROGER: What's for tea then, cheeky?

JANET: (*Proud, as if special treat.*) Tomato sauce sandwiches.

ROGER: Fucking marvellous! (*Points.*) Heinz an all!

JANET: (*Blushing.*) Only the best for our new lodger.

ROGER: You can't beat tommy sauce, especially with chips! Goes with anything. It's flexible with anything. Me mum swears by it. She has tomato sauce with everything. She'll go through what? Two, three bottles a week. But thing is right, she won't eat tomatoes as themselves, 'ts queer. (*Pause.*) You've got a good wife, Eddie. A wife men would kill for. She knows her brands.

JANET is charmed by the compliment. If ROGER only knew the truth thinks EDDIE. JANET spreads the tomato sauce on the bread.

JANET: Butter, Roger?

ROGER: I will, Jan. Cheers.

JANET spreads butter on his bread. He likes a lot of butter.

ROGER: What a lovely locket you have round yer neck, Jan.

JANET: (*Feels the locket, blushing.*) Aww thank you. Eddie bought it for me when we first met, didn't yer, Eddie? Didn't you? (*EDDIE gives a dull nod.*) It says "I love you more today than yesterday but less than tomorrow."

ROGER: (*Looks at EDDIE.*) How lovely.

EDDIE begins to eat. ROGER sees this.

ROGER: Scuse me. Are we not praying?

EDDIE: Naw, just get stuck in, chief.

ROGER: Well, I think we should pray before we settle
to eat.

JANET: (*Trying to be posh.*) Yeah, we normally pray, but
we forgot today.

EDDIE: No we sodding don't.

JANET: Yes we do. You know we do.

ROGER: Shall I start the sermon then?

JANET: If you would.

> *ROGER closes his eyes, JANET is not sure what to do, she
> copies and closes her eyes. EDDIE just watches them both,
> takes a bite of his sandwich and listens to ROGER's prayer.*

ROGER: Dear God, dear baby Jesus, thank you for putting
this food in front of useth, we are very very gratefuluth...
indeed... for this foodeth on thyeth tableuth... and I
wisheth all my loveth to your wife... Mary... All the best
... Amen.

JANET: Amen.

> *ROGER awaits EDDIE's reply.*

EDDIE: ... Amen

JANET: (*As if she prays all the time.*) That was a lovely
sermon.

ROGER: Yeah, well I always pray before tea. See, if it
weren't for God, there wouldn't be any food on this table.

JANET: That's right.

ROGER: Like, you bought it from the shop, somebody put
it on the shelf, somebody drove it to the shop, somebody

pulled it out of the ground, somebody planted the seeds so that the food would grow, but who made it grow?

JANET: Yeah, that's true, that's true that is.

ROGER: (*As if clever.*) See something made it grow.

JANET: I see what you're saying.

ROGER: That's the way my mind works. I'm querious, I query things, it's like anything, take a wasp for example, if you look at one, it looks like its arse aint connected with its head. But if you look closer – it is. It must be. It's like women an all. If I'm sitting next to one on a bus, I can always tell if it's their time of the month, I can smell it see, there's a faint taste of iron in the air, and then what I do is, I try and guess if they're wearing a jam pad or sponge cork. D' yer know what I'm saying? I'm like that. I like to look further beyond something yer know? (*Nodding, wide-eyed at his own wisdom.*) I've never wanted to be the status quo in a dire straits existence.

Silence. ROGER stops nodding and eats his sandwich. JANET and EDDIE follow suit. Much noise is made as they eat.

JANET: You're Welsh int yer, Roger?

ROGER: Born and bred, Jan.

JANET: So what brings you round this way?

ROGER: Well, yer know, personal reasons. Been in the town for about four weeks now. I've got some unfinished business to do see.

JANET: Oh right. Sounds interesting.

ROGER: (*Nodding adamantly.*) Won't be for the person I'll be finishing the business with.

JANET: So what do yer do, job like?

ROGER: Electrician, carpenter, general handyman. At the end of the day, if somebody's got something they want doing (*As if cool.*) I'll do it, know what I'm saying?

JANET: (*About EDDIE.*) He needs a job like that.

ROGER: So, what do you do, Eddie?

EDDIE: I'm...

JANET: He's on the social.

ROGER: (*Twiddles moustache.*) Oh dear. Not good.

JANET: He's always been on the social. He was born to be on the social. Aint natural for a man not to work.

EDDIE rolls his eyes back.

ROGER: That's right. I mean, if you look back at all the centuries – all the men worked, even cavemen worked. Women sat in the cave and cooked the meat they brought home. I mean, in those days, the men even dragged their girlfriends and wives around by their hair.

JANET: That's right.

ROGER finishes his tomato sauce sandwich and lets out a burp.

ROGER: (*From the Ferrero Rocher advert.*) "Excellently, with this sauce you are really spoiling us, Jan".

JANET: Good. There's more if you want it.

ROGER: (*Rubs gut.*) Not for me, Jan, thanks.

JANET: I've got pudding if you want it. (*Scrunches shoulders up, excited.*) We've got malt loaf and ice cream tonight!

ROGER: Janet, fear not, I'm full to the brim.

EDDIE: (*Eyes lit up.*) I'll have pudding, missus!

JANET: No yer not. It's your turn to do the washing up.

EDDIE: I did it last night, pal !

JANET: Listen, I've been working all day! It's the least you
can do. (*To ROGER.*) I won't have dirty pots lying
around, Roger.

ROGER: I'm just the same, Jan.

EDDIE: (*Showing off.*) Well perhaps you should get off yer
big bum once in a while then! (*To ROGER.*) 'Ave yer
seen it? When she bends over – the sun goes in!

*EDDIE laughs, looks to ROGER to join in on the "we're all men
together here" joke. ROGER just stares at him, emotionless.
EDDIE's smile disperses. He is left with an awful silence.*

JANET: (*Embarrassed in front of ROGER.*)... I beg your
pardon?

EDDIE: ... Nothing.

JANET: What... did... you... just... say?

ROGER: He said "You should get off your big bum",
I heard him.

EDDIE: I didn't say that, you must be mistaken!

ROGER: Hold on squire, hold on, there's no mistaking. You
said "big bum", now I can't mistake that with anything
else can I? Hey? "Big bun", yeah, I'll give you that,
I could have mistaken it for "big bun". But (*As if clever.*)
there aint no buns on this table.

JANET: (*Up to his face*) You don't take the mickey out of
people's bodies. I'm metaphoric. God made us all
different. He gave us all different body shapes. He gave
us different bottom shapes an all. You take people for
what they are. (*Indignant.*) I might have a big arse, but

I've got a big heart. The world would be boring if we all looked like supermodels, wouldn't it? Hey?

EDDIE: (*Thinks, genuine reply.*) No.

JANET: (*Hits him with slipper.*) Yes it bleeding would! (*Calms down, realises ROGER's there, composes herself.*) So when would yer like to move in, Roger?

ROGER: Tomorrow, if that's alright, Jan. *(Claps hands.)* I reckon we're all gonna get on like a house on fire.

JANET and ROGER smile at each other. EDDIE looks at ROGER with apprehension.

BLACKOUT.

SCENE FOUR

That next day. Saturday afternoon. The song "My Cherie Amour" by Stevie Wonder plays as ROGER moves his belongings in. He wears a cheap black plastic bodywarmer that he attained by collecting special John Player cigarette tokens. The door is open and he keeps coming in and out with various stuff like Haynes car manuals, a suitcase, a few soft porn magazines, a broken toilet seat, a pole with curtain hooks on, some taps and a cuddly toy and taking them up the stairs, whistling merrily as he does so. EDDIE sits in the armchair reading the Butlins brochure. He is obviously irritable about the door being open and ROGER moving his stuff in. He gives ROGER a dirty look every time he comes back in the house or down the stairs. ROGER is oblivious to EDDIE's mood. ROGER brings the last items in and kicks the door shut with his oxblood loafer. The music fades.

ROGER: Well that's the lot, blue! I'm gonna enjoy it here, I really am. (*EDDIE ignores him.*) A home from home,

29

that's what it is. You've got all the local amenities as well aint yer? An Happy Shopper on the corner, hairdressers, chip shop. I can see I won't be wanting for much round here.

EDDIE: ... No, you won't.

EDDIE gets up, goes into the kitchen and looks in a cupboard. ROGER starts to get stuff out of a box. EDDIE comes out of the kitchen.

EDDIE: You aint seen those coconut creams anywhere, have yer?

ROGER: What, McVities ones?

EDDIE: Yeah.

ROGER: Big packet?

EDDIE: Yeah.

ROGER: Twenny-nine p ones?

EDDIE: (*Excited.*) Yeah, they're the ones!

ROGER: I eat 'em.

EDDIE pauses, looks pissed off. He goes back into the kitchen in a huff.

EDDIE: I suppose I'll have to have a bourbon cream instead then. (*Sticks head out of kitchen.*) Sharnt a?

ROGER: You can't – I've had those as well.

EDDIE is really pissed off. He goes to say something but stops himself. He sits back down. He picks up the Butlins brochure and flaps it about to make clear of his mood to ROGER. ROGER gets out a hammer and starts hammering a nail into the wall. EDDIE watches with his mouth open.

EDDIE: Scuse me, pal! Scuse me!

ROGER: (*Stops.*) Yeah?

EDDIE: What yer doing?

ROGER: (*Pause.*) What d'yer mean?

EDDIE: What yer doing with me wall?

ROGER: (*Confused.*) Well, what d'yer think I'm doing? I'm putting a nail in.

EDDIE: You can't just start hammering nails into me wall.

ROGER: (*Dumbfounded.*) Well why not? How else am I gonna put me knick-knacks up?

ROGER starts hammering again.

EDDIE: Whoa whoa whoa whoa whoa, you'll knock the bloody wall down!

ROGER: How else am I gonna put me picture up?

EDDIE: It's plaster is that, you'll bring the house down.

ROGER: Listen, I'm only happy when I've got me pictures up. And you just don't want me to be happy.

EDDIE: Well put it up upstairs in yer bedroom.

ROGER: It aint the same.

EDDIE: Well you can't put it up there.

ROGER: Listen grandad, I AM NOT gonna bring the house down.

EDDIE: (*Flaps brochure open.*) Well you do what yer want then. No skin off my nose. I just live here!

ROGER bows and then continues the hammering. He finishes putting the nail in. Then, he reaches inside his box

31

and proudly gets out a cheap and nasty picture of a red Ferrari parked in view of the Golden Gate bridge. EDDIE watches him hang it up then resumes reading. ROGER stands back, admires, and adjusts it. ROGER looks at EDDIE to see if he's impressed. EDDIE is not looking. ROGER's smile disperses. He reaches into his box, gets out a similarly cheap and nasty picture, picks up a nail, looks at EDDIE, then, thinking that if he bangs the nail into the wall quicker and harder, EDDIE won't notice. He starts hammering again.

EDDIE: Whoa whoa whoa whoa whoa!

ROGER: What now?

EDDIE: How many bloody pictures are yer putting up?

ROGER: I aint sure yet. I'm gonna play it by ear.

EDDIE: C'mon, I aint gonna have pictures everywhere. You can have that one up there, but no more chief.

ROGER: Well I'm about to put a Porsche up.

EDDIE: No more, please.

ROGER: Listen grandad, I can't just have a Ferrari Tesseroti up there, I've gotta have a Porsche Spider as well, know what I'm saying?

EDDIE: Well put yer Porsche up upstairs.

ROGER: I can't, because I won't see them both together then... will I?

EDDIE: I'm not gonna argue you with yer, Roger.

ROGER: What yer doing now then?

EDDIE: I'm talking to yer, not arguing with yer.

ROGER: Listen, why are you giving me a hard time?

EDDIE: I'm not giving you a hard time...

ROGER: (*Interrupts.*) Nothing I do ever seems to please you, does it? I mean, all I wanna do right? All I wanna do is see my Ferrari and my Porsche and you won't let me see them! I'm only happy when I've got me pictures up and you just want me to be miserable for the rest of me life!

EDDIE pauses, confused, as he suddenly realises there must be one short at the nuthouse. ROGER turns around and continues to bang the nail into the wall with much ferocity and anger. EDDIE has given up. He doesn't want to set ROGER off. He just watches him trying to fathom him out. ROGER hangs the picture on the wall. He picks up his box, heads for the stairs.

ROGER: (*Long pause.*) I'm happy now.

ROGER goes up the stairs. He slams his bedroom door shut.

EDDIE looks around, perplexed. He gives out a sigh, and quietly resumes reading the Butlins brochure. There is peace in the air again. Then, suddenly and without warning, "In the Summertime" by Mungo Jerry plays at full belt from ROGER's bedroom. EDDIE nearly jumps out of his seat. He holds his heart. The song's muffled bass belches through the walls. EDDIE looks up at the ceiling. He throws down the brochure and heads up the stairs. He can just about be heard knocking on ROGER's door and shouting but it is locked and ROGER is not replying. EDDIE comes back downstairs. He storms off into the hallway, then the music grinds to a halt. EDDIE comes back out holding a fuse from the fuse box. He looks up at the ceiling in celebration and sits back down in the armchair. ROGER comes down the stairs. EDDIE quickly gets up, ready for a confrontation. But ROGER just goes into the kitchen, whistling the song he was playing. He goes through the fridge. EDDIE prepares himself to ask ROGER to vacate the premises. ROGER comes out of the kitchen with a tin of fruit cocktail. He sits on the sofa.

ROGER: (*Eating from the tin.*) I think there's something wrong with yer electricity, grandad.

EDDIE: Oi! What yer doing? That's for bloody tea!

ROGER: I'm fucking hungry!

EDDIE: That's for pudding is that!

ROGER: Oh well pardon me if I didn't know there was a food embargo on!

EDDIE: (*Puts his hands over his head.*) God almighty.

ROGER: Oh! That reminds me, I found twenny quid in yer coat pocket this afternoon.

EDDIE: Yer what?

ROGER: You've got more money than sense, Eddie – leaving money lying around like that.

EDDIE: (*In disbelief.*) What?

ROGER: (*Lifts foot up.*) Nice socks an all. I'm a bugger for odd socks and stuff, so I took a few of yours. I didn't take the ones with snowmen on. They must be yer Christmas ones. I thought I'd leave you them.

EDDIE: (*Sarcastic.*) That's kind of yer.

ROGER: Well, yer know, I didn't wanna take advantage or anything. (*Munching on the fruit cocktail.*) How long you an yer missus been living here then? Looks like you need a new paint job, no, don't get me wrong or anything, I like it here. (*Winks.*) Your missus is a bit of a character aint she? Hey? Goes on a bit don't she? No, don't get me wrong, I like her. Go for the big birds then,

Eddie? Like 'em big do yer? Hey? Don't sweat much for a fat lass does she? Scrubs up well an all. (*Sips the juice from can.*) What about those bras? Hey? Eddie? Bet yer could Chinook tanks out with those fuckers.

EDDIE: That's my missus you're talking about.

ROGER: I'm only having a laugh, grandad! Don't take it all personal like. I wunt mind a bit meself. I'd love to get a pair of scissors and cut out a square out of the arse bit in her leggings and sellotape it to me nose. Know what I'm saying? (*Looks in tin.*) You don't get many cherries in these do yer?

EDDIE: (*Sits down.*) Listen, Roger. I've been thinking like, yer know, thinking. And what I was thinking was... (*Pause.*) I don't think it's gonna work out, I mean, don't get me wrong or anything, I think you're a smashing lad but I think it's best you went.

ROGER: (*Points, laughs, thinks it's a joke.*) Nice one, Eddie, nice one.

ROGER continues with his fruit cocktail.

EDDIE: No, Roger, listen to me lad, it's not gonna work out. I'm sure you'll find somewhere else to go.

ROGER: (*Pause.*) What you trying to say to me, Eddie?

EDDIE: Well, I'm asking yer to leave, Roger. I'm sorry. That's just the way it is.

ROGER: (*Looking around in disbelief.*) What have a done?

EDDIE: You haven't done anything, it just isn't gonna work.

ROGER: But I've only been here a couple of hours!

EDDIE: I'm sorry, chief. That's just the way the cookie crumbles sometimes.

ROGER: You can't just kick me out. I mean, I haven't got no family or anything. I aint got anywhere to go to.

EDDIE: You've got yer mum.

ROGER: Yeah. (*Pause.*) But I thought we were getting on famously, us two. Having a joke and all that. I mean, that's why I wanted to stay here because I felt, yer know, I felt I was part of the family.

EDDIE: Listen lad, you're gonna have to wash yer ears out, you're not listening to me are yer?

ROGER: Well I'm in shock, I can't believe it. It feels like a whole bleeding nightmare.

EDDIE: Look, I'll let yer come back at Christmas, you can pop in for a glass of sherry and a mince pie.

ROGER: But I aint finished my fruit cocktail or anything yet.

EDDIE: Look, you can take the fruit cocktail with yer. It's best if there's no hard goodbyes hey? So if you wanna start taking yer car pictures down and stuff...

ROGER: (*Slams down tin.*) You've never liked me have yer?

EDDIE: What?

ROGER: If you liked me, you wunt chuck me out. (*Pointing at him with the spoon.*) Cause I take that kind of stuff personally, Eddie.

EDDIE: Listen lad, if you don't go, I'll have to call the police.

ROGER: But I'll come back.

EDDIE: You won't, cause they'll restrain yer with one of their orders.

ROGER slowly gets up. Stares at EDDIE, then pinches his glasses.

EDDIE: Oi! Give 'em back you bleeder!

ROGER: Give what back?

EDDIE: Me glasses!

EDDIE tries to get the glasses. Everything is a blur. He tries to catch ROGER but it is useless. ROGER enjoys himself.

ROGER: Where's he going?

EDDIE: Give 'em back!

ROGER: Don't know what yer talking about.

EDDIE: (*Reaching out.*) I'll get cross!

ROGER: You wanna get yer glasses first!

EDDIE: You won't like me when I'm cross! (*Does a feeble attempt at a karate manoeuvre.*) I'm a black belt me.

ROGER laughs as EDDIE spreads his legs and does karate chops at thin air.

ROGER: Yeah! You look like it!

EDDIE gives up trying to look hard and tries to grab his glasses. ROGER moves out of his way.

ROGER: Aww aww, look, I wonder whose glasses these are? Perhaps I should throw 'em in the bin.

EDDIE: I'm not playing silly buggers with you all afternoon! Give 'em back!

ROGER goes around the room pretending the glasses are an aeroplane, making aeroplane noises. EDDIE falls over the sofa.

ROGER: Oi! Mr Magoo – this way!

EDDIE: Give me 'em back you little bleeder!

ROGER: After you've played 'Find my glasses.'

EDDIE: I don't wanna play 'Find my bleeding glasses!'

ROGER pushes him into the armchair and stands over him. His eyes bulge out of their sockets. EDDIE suddenly feels very uncomfortable.

ROGER: I'll come back, you won't know when or where I'll come back, but I will. You could wake up one dark night and you'll see me standing at the bottom of your bed, and if I don't come into your room, I'll come into your nightmares. (*Leans over.*) And you'll have to take sleeping tablets and stuff because you'll never be able to escape me and I'll put curses on you, I'll voodoo you up something bad and everywhere you go you'll see little pygmies with green hair watching you, first they'll be one, then another, then they'll be a whole lot of 'em and then, (*Right up to his face.*) whilst you're asleep they'll climb into yer gob and they'll haunt your innards for eternity and you'll hear them screaming inside you and they'll try to find their way out and you'll see their fingers and elbows pushing out of your skin, and they'll keep fighting their way out, fighting, fighting, until one day you FUCKING EXPLODE!

EDDIE has gone as far back in his seat as he can.

EDDIE: Oh c'mon Roger, there's no need for all that to happen. I'm only asking you to leave.

ROGER: Well I aint going. (*Long pause.*) Me, you, Jan. Just one big happy family. (*ROGER pats EDDIE's glasses back on to his nose.*) Cunt.

One could cut the tension with a knife. As the tension between the two rises and EDDIE fears for his life, JANET comes in from work. Her entrance dispels the silence. ROGER's voice and mannerisms suddenly change. He is charming and polite. EDDIE is in a quiet shock.

ROGER: Evening, Jan!

JANET: Hi Roger! Have yer moved all yer stuff in?

ROGER: Just about, blue, just about!

JANET: (*Hangs up coat.*) I hope Eddie's made yer welcome.

ROGER: He has. Made me very welcome didn't yer, Eddie?

EDDIE gives a disconnected nod. He is still pressed up against his seat.

ROGER: (*Claps hands.*) Fancy a cuppa, blue?

JANET: Don't worry, I'll make it.

ROGER: No, you sit yerself down, blue. You put yer feet up.

ROGER goes into the kitchen and puts the kettle on.

JANET: Aww lovely. (*Sits down on sofa.*) It's lovely to have someone make you a cup of tea when yer come in. (*To EDDIE, still in shock.*) You don't do that for me do yer?

ROGER: (*Shouting out.*) Enjoy it, Jan, you deserve it!

JANET: You spoil me rotten you do.

ROGER: Rubissssssshhh. Lady like you deserves spoiling!

JANET: (*About EDDIE.*) What's up with mardy chops?

ROGER: (*In kitchen doorway.*) I dunno, Jan, he's been like it since I got here.

JANET: Has he been out looking for work?

ROGER: Naww, just sat there.

JANET: (*To EDDIE.*) I suppose yer proud of yerself.

ROGER: For a man who receives Job Seeker's Allowance Jan – I can't see much seeking being done.

JANET shakes her head. ROGER goes back into kitchen to make the tea. As JANET takes off her shoes and rubs her sweaty feet, EDDIE tries to grab her attention. He keeps coughing. She looks up, EDDIE gestures about ROGER, puts his finger to head, swivels it and mouths 'nutter'. JANET doesn't understand. He keeps doing it, she screws her face up. Then she gets it.

JANET: Nutter? Who's a nutter?

ROGER comes in with the mug of tea.

ROGER: What's that, Jan?

JANET: Awww tea, lovely.

ROGER gives her the tea and sits down next to her.

ROGER: Been busy, blue?

JANET: I've been on me feet all day, Roger.

ROGER: Aww you've not.

JANET: Well Joyce was off, so I had to do one of her wards, then I had to help Carol out with the sheets cause somebody'd had a coughing fit and touched cloth. Honestly Roger, I aint had a minute to meself.

ROGER: Jan – you just let yer body crash out.

JANET: I shall have to. (*Sips tea.*) Aww lovely tea, Roger.

ROGER: Well I get it from me mam, she knows how to make good tea. And there aint no tea like a woman's tea.

JANET: True that.

ROGER: Hold on a sec, I've got a surprise for yer.

ROGER reaches behind the sofa and presents a box of Terry's All Gold. JANET'S eyes light up.

ROGER: Gold for the lady?

JANET: Awww you shunt have!

ROGER: Just a little something to celebrate many happy years together.

JANET: Awww lovely, they're my favourite too!

ROGER: Read yer mind didn't a? Every woman loves All Gold.

ROGER offers her the box. JANET is excited trying to decide what to choose. She wiggles her fingers above the chocolates and rubs her feet together in anticipation. She takes a soft centre.

ROGER: I knew you'd like that one!

JANET: (*Savours the taste.*) Aww heaven. I do like a soft centre.

ROGER: (*In a sickeningly bad American accent.*) "Life is like a box of chocolates, you never know what you're gonna get". Have you seen that film, cheeky?

JANET: The one with that daft American chap in?

ROGER: That's the one! Made me cry that film did. I like films about people and their humanities

JANET: I've got a gump here, you can watch him for free.

ROGER and JANET laugh. EDDIE just watches them both, wary of ROGER. ROGER offers her another one.

JANET: Aww I shouldn't, Roger, I'm being ever so naughty.

ROGER: Go onnnnnnn gel, tek a bleddy chocolate. You only live once.

JANET takes one, puts it in her mouth. She scrunches her shoulders up and smiles at ROGER. ROGER takes one himself, returns the smile. ROGER takes one, then looks at

EDDIE, opens his mouth so that EDDIE can see all the mush on his tongue.

ROGER: You're husband to be's very quiet, Jan.

JANET: (*Mouth full of chocolate.*) He's always quiet. He's got nothing interesting to say.

ROGER: He must have something to say, surely.

JANET: No, not really.

ROGER: Perhaps he's just shy, Jan.

JANET: Stupid more like. I reckon it was that time we went to Blackpool, this mule kicked him in the head. (*Sups up tea.*) Right, I better go and change, it's always nice to slip into something more comfy when you come in from work.

ROGER: Tell me about it!

JANET: I like to come in, Roger, get me slippers on, have a coffee, a sandwich and a wee.

ROGER: I'm just the same, Jan. (*Rubbing hands together.*) So what's for tea tonight, cheeky?

JANET: Aww just help yerself, Roger. Eddie'll make you something. We've got jam on Jacob's cream crackers tonight!

JANET exits upstairs. ROGER watches her go, then he turns to EDDIE, smiles. EDDIE's face is filled with horror.

ROGER: You heard her! Go in the kitchen and make me a sandwich. I'm hungry.

EDDIE: Listen, Roger, I won't charge yer for...

ROGER: Don't get intellectual with me you four-eyed fucker. Go on the kitchen and make me a sandwich up yer cunt.

EDDIE: Please Roger, I'll even pay yer to leave if...

ROGER: (*Clicks fingers.*) Now!

EDDIE doesn't know what to do. He gives in, slowly gets up and backs off into the kitchen. EDDIE makes a sandwich. He looks at ROGER and the round of bread, then he wipes the bread across the floor, then spits in it. He breathes over the bread more, gobs in it and licks it. He comes back in and places the sandwich in front of ROGER. He sits down and waits for ROGER's response.

ROGER: Tell yer what, Eddie. (*Winks, holds out plate.*) You can have it instead.

EDDIE: Naww, you have it, Roger.

ROGER: What's up? There's nothing wrong with it is there?

EDDIE: No.

ROGER: Well I suggest you eat it then. (*Stares at him.*) Don't wanna go wasting God's food do we?

EDDIE: No, Roger.

ROGER walks over to him, gives him the sandwich.

ROGER: I don't like gob in my sandwiches Eddie.(*Winks.*) 'Enjoy'.

ROGER stands over him and watches EDDIE put the sandwich slowly in his mouth. He pretends to enjoy it. ROGER quickly changes persona again as JANET comes back down the stairs. She wears a frilly skirt and a blouse reserved for best occasions. She has put more make-up on and overdone it on the rouge. EDDIE nearly chokes on the sandwich.

ROGER: What a lovely dress, Jan! Go on, giv' us a twirl!

JANET does a little shy twirl. ROGER claps. Encouraged, she does another. ROGER claps again and shouts 'Ole!'. EDDIE just watches her with bits of sandwich in the corner of his mouth. JANET is clearly enjoying herself. She twirls around once more and falls back onto the sofa next to ROGER.

ROGER: You should be one of them flamingo dancers, Jan!

JANET: Well I used to do alot of dancing years ago, Roger!

ROGER: Well you've got it in the foot work, Jan. (*Looks at her feet.*) D'yer know it's the first time I've noticed, you've got lovely feet, Jan.

JANET: Gerrout!

ROGER: Yeah you have, you've got feet an angel'd be proud of. Did yer know yer can always tell a woman by her feet?

EDDIE just stares at them both, despising ROGER.

JANET: (*Giggly.*) What do they say about me?

ROGER: (*Nudges her.*) Aww that'd be telling!

They laugh. EDDIE is not amused.

ROGER: Tell yer what, whip yer tights off gel and I'll give 'em a massage.

JANET: No, I couldn't.

ROGER: Go on gel, you'll feel better for it.

JANET: I couldn't let yer, really.

ROGER: Go on, treat yerself, let yer hair down once in a while!

JANET pauses, then excitedly takes off her tights. EDDIE doesn't believe what he is seeing. ROGER takes her foot, massages it. JANET is oblivious to EDDIE's mood.

JANET: (*To EDDIE.*) You won't do that for me, will yer? Rub me feet?

ROGER works on her feet. JANET closes her eyes. EDDIE is on the verge of exploding. His face has gone red. ROGER works on JANET's other foot. ROGER gives EDDIE a look of 'I know how to treat a woman good'.

JANET: Aww that's lovely, Roger.

ROGER: You enjoy it, Jan.

JANET: Aww heaven... aww yeah... heaven... yeah... right just there... uhmmm... uhmmmm... uhmmm.

Suddenly EDDIE slams down the plate on the floor and stands up.

EDDIE: LEAVE... HER... FEET... ALONE!

JANET: Oi! Oi oi oi oi!

ROGER: Sorry?

EDDIE: You heard pal.

ROGER: (*Lets go of JANET's foot.*) I'm sorry Jan, I mean, whoa whoa, I don't wanna cause any arguments here. (*Gets up.*) Perhaps I should go, I don't think me and yer loved one are getting on.

JANET: You sit yerself down!

EDDIE: (*Feeling brave.*) Piss off out this house before I throw yer out!

EDDIE spreads his legs and rolls up his sleeves in a weak attempt to frighten ROGER.

JANET: Roger, sit yerself down, yer going nowhere.

ROGER: I think I'll retire to my room. I know where I'm not wanted.

ROGER exits upstairs, pulling a hurt face.

JANET: See what you've done now! Upsetting people!

EDDIE: I want him out by tomorrow morning! The bloke's a bloody nutter! He's nicked money off me, he's physically threatened me with evil spirits, he's got a screw loose in his head!

JANET: You should be ashamed of yourself.

EDDIE: (*Holds head in despair.*) I'm telling the truth!

JANET: You're nought but a liar, you'll do anything to get yer own way!

EDDIE: Well if he aint going, I'm going, pal. How's that suit yer?

JANET: (*Nods him towards door.*) Go on then.

EDDIE: (*Pause.*) What?

EDDIE can't believe what he is hearing. He's not sure if she's serious or not.

EDDIE: ... Right, alright, I'm off then.

EDDIE goes to walk away. He walks heavily to make a point of it.

EDDIE: I mean it, I'm going, you won't see me again.

JANET: See yer then!

EDDIE puts his coat on, doing the buttons up slowly to give JANET time to change her mind, then he gives her one last look, and exits. JANET gives a knowing smile. Twenty seconds pass, EDDIE comes back in, hangs his coat up, sits back down in a huff. JANET gives him a look of 'I know you too well'. EDDIE looks upwards for divine intervention.

BLACKOUT.

SCENE FIVE

*The next day. Sunday morning. "Never on a Sunday"
by Lynne Cormell plays. Whilst JANET is at work and
ROGER is out, EDDIE calmly and contentedly places
ROGER's suitcase and other belongings outside the door. He
whistles merrily as he does so. He goes upstairs and brings
down ROGER's porn magazines. He flicks through one,
engrossed, smiles excitedly at one particular picture. He places
them outside. He goes back up and brings down a cuddly toy,
the broken toilet seat and a broken curtain rail, puts them
outside. He takes down the cheap and nasty car pictures,
throws them out of the door and with a pair of pliers, he pulls
out the nails. It's as if the nails have become the very thorns
in EDDIE's side. He has never looked so happy. He rubs his
hands in self-congratulation and shuts the door. He locks it.
But suddenly to his horror, he turns around to see ROGER
standing in the kitchen entrance watching him with his large
and cumbersome head. He carries a bin liner with stuff
inside and wears a T-shirt with a pig on top of another pig,
with the caption "makin' bacon" written underneath.*

ROGER: Problem?

EDDIE: (*Stutters.*) No, no problems at all. (*Smiles.*)
Everything's all hunky-dory, Roger.

ROGER: So if everything's all hunky-dory, Eddie, perhaps
you can tell me why all my fashion garments and all my
belongings are lying outside. (*EDDIE doesn't know what
to say.*) I suppose your hands just accidentally picked my
stuff up and threw it outside did they? (*EDDIE nods.*)
What, just like I saw you 'accidentally' go into the police
station last night?`

EDDIE: I didn't mean to chuck 'em out, honestly. You can
forgive me, you're a religious man!

ROGER: Oh right, I'll forget the whole incident shall a? I'll just walk into the sunset with all my belongings with mud all over 'em and pretend nothing happened shall a? (*EDDIE gives him a hopeful nod.*) If everybody forgived Eddie, nobody'd get anything done would they? There'd be no prisons, no correction centres, no courts, no policemen, no nothing. There'd be chaos everywhere wunt there? People would be nicking things out of shop windows and upsetting everyone wunt they? (*EDDIE nods.*) Well you've upset me for a long, long time Eddie, and now you've upset my belongings. I wanted to see what you were *really* like, see if you'd changed. I tried to give you a second chance. But you didn't take it, did you?

EDDIE: I don't know what yer mean.

ROGER: Oh yes you do. I've been looking forward to this for a very, very, very long time.

EDDIE: (*Not looking forward to it.*) Why?

ROGER: Cause you and me have something to sort out.

EDDIE: (*Scared.*) Do we?

ROGER: Oh yes indeedy.

EDDIE tries to get out of the door but ROGER closes in. EDDIE retreats. ROGER bolts the door. He gets JANET's tights that are hanging next to the window and approaches EDDIE, tugging angrily at the tights.

EDDIE: Look, I've never met you before, there's nothing to sort out!

ROGER: Oh yes you have. Siddown.

EDDIE: Look (*Gets out wallet.*) if it's money yer want, then take this, chief! It's not a lot but take it!

ROGER: I want something else. Siddown

EDDIE: Well take the TV, take the sofa, take anything yer want!

ROGER: SIDDOWN!

EDDIE sits down at the table. ROGER ties him up with the tights. EDDIE is too frightened to struggle free.

EDDIE: (*Babbling.*) Listen, Roger, if you start any more funny business... I shall have to bring me mates round... aww they're ever such big lads... (*ROGER ignores him, tying him up.*) One's a wrestler! He is! Yeah!... Does a wicked Boston Crab!... Don't say I didn't warn yer... (*ROGER finishes tying him up. He fetches the bin liner and places it on the table. He rummages through it.*) The other's a boxer... He is. Big black bloke... World heavyweight champion he is!... Eight times... 30 KO's... Waugh aww don't say I dint warn yer... They'll come round and...

ROGER: SHUT THE FUCK UP!

ROGER carefully brings out a funeral urn and places it on the table. It is clear that it is a prized possession.

ROGER: Recognise that?

EDDIE: Never seen it before, pal.

ROGER: Do you know what it is?

EDDIE: (*Squints.*) Well it's a vase int it?

ROGER: No, Eddie. It's a urn.

EDDIE: A what?

ROGER: An urn. Do you know what you use an urn for, Eddie?

EDDIE: Put a dead person's ash in?

ROGER: That's right.

EDDIE: Oh. So, is there a dead person's ash in there then?

ROGER: Oh yeah.

EDDIE: Oh. (*Pause.*) And who might that be then?

ROGER: You don't know?

EDDIE: Course I don't know!

ROGER: Well I'll tell you who it is, since you don't know. That, in there, those ashes are my mum's.

EDDIE: But you said...

ROGER: (*Interrupts.*) Well I lied!

EDDIE: Oh dear. Sorry to hear about that, pal.

ROGER: Yeah.

EDDIE: Did she pass away shortly?

ROGER: Shortly, yeah.

EDDIE: Oh dear, sorry to hear it. What she die of?

ROGER: Cancer. Lung cancer. It was terrible, to tell the truth it was a nightmare, yer know, to see her fighting for breath.

EDDIE: Phhhhhhh. I can imagine, pal.

ROGER: Oh you can, can you?

EDDIE: Yeah. Must have been terrible for yer.

ROGER: (*Sarcastic.*) Thanks Eddie, for yer concern.

EDDIE: (*Winks*) I'm a very caring person you see.

ROGER: Oh is that right?

EDDIE: (*Smiles.*) Yeah.

ROGER: Well if you're so fucking caring, then you'll obviously be upset to find out that's your fucking wife in there! The wife you left and never gave a penny to! The wife you never visited when she was fucking dying! The wife who sent you letters that you never returned! That's who, Eddie! THAT'S WHO'S IN THE FUCKING URN!

EDDIE suddenly sees a fan and some shit heading towards it.

EDDIE: (*Long pause.*) Right.

Then ROGER takes off his hair piece and throws it on the floor. He is completely bald underneath except for some gingery greasy tufts around the back.

ROGER: And if you're still so fucking caring, then you're obviously pleased to meet your son, aren't you, Eddie? The son you walked out on when I was nine! The son, Eddie, the son you aint gave a fuck about for the past twenny-five years!

EDDIE: But you're Welsh! My Roger wasn't from Wales.

ROGER: Well thanks to you we had to move there after our house was fucking repossessed didn't we?!

EDDIE: Oh dear.

ROGER: Yeah 'Oh dear'. I've been trying to track you down you miserable little cunt for the past seven months. I couldn't believe me luck when I followed you to the Post Office.

EDDIE: It was you then! I could see yer, I knew you were behind me!

ROGER: Yeah it was me. Thought it was my birthday I did when you put the ad for your room in the window!

Thought it was Christmas! Cause I've been watching you Eddie, watching you a lot. I thought I'd get to know yer a bit before we met formally. See if you weren't as bad as I'd always thought you to be. And even 30 years on, you still don't want me. Even when I showed you my car pictures, you weren't impressed. I thought you'd be proud of me, I thought you'd see what a brilliant bloke I'd turned out to be. But all you've given me is grief.

EDDIE: How did you find me?

ROGER: How did I find you? Not that many E. Turners in the phone book is there? (*Sarcastic.*) Only about five thousand in one hundred phone books, but when I got this address, it looked the type of house I'd imagine you live in, and when I saw you put the rubbish out that night, I thought it can't be him can it? And it was. Bit unfortunate for you I suppose, but me, well, fucking hell, I could hardly retain my excitement.

EDDIE: It wasn't me who walked out, she drove me out!

ROGER: That's convenient.

EDDIE: It's true, Roger!

ROGER: You left! And you left with the radio, me mum's savings, and me mum's jewellery you thieving bastard!

EDDIE: You've got it all wrong!

ROGER: Are you trying to say my mum was a liar?

EDDIE: No! She's sounds like she's got herself muddled up!

ROGER: Well she aint got herself muddled up anymore has she? Cause the poor sod's dead! She's ashes now int she? Ashes!

EDDIE: Listen Roger, listen to me, yer mum was going loony, I had to get out. She thought I was the devil,

Roger! She used to splash holy water on me whilst I was asleep, she even use to throw ashtrays at me head!

ROGER: You're worse than the devil.

EDDIE: It's true, she wasn't the full ticket, Roger. She thought there were demons in the cellar! She was heading for the cracker factory, son. I was gonna come back but the longer I left it, the harder it was!

ROGER: But you dint did you? Didn't you even think about how we would feel?

EDDIE: I know it's been hard for yer, Roger, I know it's ...

ROGER: Hard? Hard? You can't even begin to imagine how we felt. You can't even begin to apprehend how we felt. You can't even begin to feel the slightest, smallest, tiniest bit of how we felt, cause between you and me – when I found out you'd planned the whole fucking thing and left without even a goodbye and took my tin with three-and-a-half years worth of spending money in it – I was positively frothing man!

EDDIE: Son – I can understand you feeling like this. (*As if a counsellor.*) I really can. The emotions you're feeling Roger are quite natural for somebody who's gone through what you've been through.

ROGER: Are they? That's kind of yer to allow me those feelings, Eddie, it really is. Cause apart from taking my spending money (*Gets out old piece of paper from his pocket, reads it.*) you took my mum's jewellery, her purse, 'Spot the Ball' money that mum always left near the door, one weekend bag with a small tear at the bottom, one green suitcase with steel frame and padlock, my leopard-skin wallet which, fortunate for me, only contained my free school-dinner card and a bus receipt, one travel alarm clock with floral interface and snooze facility, one Kodak

Polaroid camera, two, and I repeat – two antique silver candle holders, one mother and baby crystal dolphin clock, a nine carat Hugs & Kisses fancy bracelet, two silver and gold clown earrings, one silver locket reading (*Slight irony.*) 'I love you more today than yesterday but less than tomorrow', which should have read 'I love you less today than I did yesterday and even less tomorrow', four dinner mats with pictures of Shire horses on, one brass picture-frame, and last but not least and by no means not the last – a 33cl bottle of Brut fucking 33! (*Just staring at him.*) Makes interesting reading doesn't it, Eddie?

EDDIE: *(Not sure what to say.)* I never had those dinner mats! But I'll make it up to yer...

ROGER: You'll never be able to make up for what you've done. At school, the kids called me a bastard, I used to dread it, walking through those big black metal gates in the morning where they would be waiting for me, the sky would be yellow and grey and you wunt believe how low I was for an nine-year-old. They would tear my hood off my coat or hit me with their belts when the teacher wasn't there, or they'd gob in my face or make me lie in dogshit, if they didn't call me a bastard, they called me flea bag or lurgy or leper. Mum couldn't afford new clothes, so I never told her about the rips in my trousers or in my coat, I would sit in my bedroom and sow them up myself. Everyday, I thought you might come back, I would imagine you walk up that garden path and you'd look up and see me at the bedroom window and as you'd come through that front door, things would be normal again. The sun would come back, Christmas would be a time to look forward to and I would never have to hear mam crying downstairs all the time and listening to that fucking song every five minutes But you never came did

you? You never walked up that path did you? You just
walked right out of our lives, gone, as if you never
existed, as if we didn't either. I wanted to find you, I
wanted to see what you had to say, it was heart-breaking
to watch her die, it killed me Eddie, it really fucking
killed me. And where were you? You weren't by her
bedside, you weren't holding her hand, you weren't
telling her everything's gonna be okay and God'll look
after her. But the more hurt I felt then, the more I would
make you pay, and now I don't have to cry anymore.
Because it's your turn now, Eddie, it's your turn to do
the crying.

EDDIE: (*In desperation.*) I'll tell yer what son. How about
you leave us yer address and telephone number?

ROGER: (*Blinking.*) Yeah, go on.

EDDIE: (*Happy with own idea.*) And I'll send you a card on
yer birthday with a tenner in. How about that?

ROGER: How generous of yer, but no thanks.

EDDIE: I've got valuables. I've got a watch!

ROGER: A watch?

EDDIE: Yeah, it's Seiko, it's a good un.

ROGER: After trying to find you for seven-and-a-half
months, travelled the wedth and breadth of the country,
I've spent over a thousand pounds in petrol and
accommodation, spent 24 years, seven months, and three
days planning for the day to meet you, do you really
think I'm gonna forget everything by receiving a
FUCKING SEIKO WATCH?

EDDIE: (*Thinks about it.*) Yeah. It's got an alarm on it.

ROGER: I don't care if it's got a fucking alarm on it!

EDDIE: Well I've got other stuff. I've got a suit and a cardigan you can have!

ROGER: A suit! Do you really think I'd wanna be seen dead wearing one of your horrible grey flannel suits!

EDDIE: Alright, I've got some albums you might like! Val Doonican, Patsy Cline, Stereo Galaxy!

ROGER: Val fucking Doonican, you've gotta be kidding!

EDDIE: No, I'm not, I'm deadly serious. (*Excited.*) Tell you what, I'll throw in Andy Williams as well.

ROGER: No no no no, you've got it all wrong, Eddie, I don't want songs.

EDDIE: I've got books! One's a Bible. You're a God-fearing man!

ROGER draws the curtains, and a darkness falls upon the room. EDDIE is filled with a sickening fear.

EDDIE: (*Panicky.*) Oh c'mon Roger ... son. Listen to yer dad. You've got it all wrong, things just didn't work out between us, these things happen! I wrote letters but you and Irene'd gone, I even sent yer birthday cards with postal orders in, I never forgot yer son, I thought about yer everyday of me life! I just didn't know where you were. If I knew, I would have come for yer lad, I would. (*Winks happily.*) Yer dad would have come for yer.

ROGER rummages through his bin liner. EDDIE dreads to think what might be in there. ROGER carefully gets out a hospital gown, a pair of women's shoes, a Brenda Lee album, spectacles in a case, a pair of well-worn slippers, an hearing aid, a framed picture of EDDIE and IRENE's wedding day but EDDIE has been torn from the picture, and a lock of grey hair. He lays them down onto the table with care and admiration. EDDIE looks at his wife's items. ROGER goes over to stereo and puts on the Brenda Lee album. He plays "All Alone Am I". ROGER lights a fag, looks at EDDIE. He goes back over to the table. He looks solemnly at all the items, particularly the picture.

ROGER: You never kissed my mum once did you, Eddie?

EDDIE: (*Adamant.*) Yeah I did, I did. I did all the while!

ROGER: That aint what she told me. You never gave her one loving kiss.

EDDIE: I didn't like kissing! She always had a woodbine in her mouth!

ROGER: (*Holds the picture in front of him.*) You can kiss her now then can't yer?

EDDIE: Roger, please, let's sit down and talk about this – father to son!

ROGER: KISS ME FUCKING MUM!

EDDIE kisses the photo. He does it several times. Then ROGER kisses it, puts it down and leans it gently against the urn so that him and EDDIE can see his mother.

ROGER: D'you know what the strangest thing was before she died? The last thing she managed to eat was some strawberries and ice cream, only a little taste cause she was very ill see. It was matron's treat cause Wimbledon was on the telly, so matron bought all the cancer patients strawberries. Lovely she was. Bit like Jan. Yer know? Got it in here, in her heart. So, after mam died, matron gave me all her belongings in a little see-through bag. She didn't have a lot of stuff me mam, just stuff you'd have if you were old. And in this bag was some bits and bobs and her teeth, false teeth. So when I got home, I looked at these teeth and guess what I found? Little strawberry pips 'round the gum bits. Weird int it? The fact that she'd eaten them strawberries whilst watching the semi-final. And she didn't know that she would die later that night. Weird. Don't you think?

EDDIE: ... Yes, Roger.

ROGER picks up the slippers, he smells them.

ROGER: I think these are strange too, d'yer know why? (*Eddie shakes his head, concerned.*) Cause they smell of death. Fucking dreadful smell. Bit like cats' arseholes and rotting corn beef and when they trolled 'em off her feet, I could smell old age and agony and pain and the end of everything.

The song finishes. ROGER looks solemnly at all the items on the table.

EDDIE: (*Genuine.*) I'm sorry.

ROGER: (*Picks up pliers EDDIE used earlier.*) Bit too late for apologies, don't you think? (*Studying pliers.*) What d'yer reckon, Eddie? An eye for an eye, a tooth for a tooth? A tooth for every five years since you walked out? (*Looks at ceiling, reckons up.*) I make that just over five teeth, Eddie. (*Winks.*) But we'll call it six shall we?

EDDIE: (*Begins to cry.*) If you kill me I'll come back and haunt yer like you've done me! I'll make your life hell! God can see what you're doing!

ROGER: There aint no God, Eddie. Cause you're going down there, under the floorboards to see the man with the horns on his head, and he's gonna get the biggest and the hottest pitchfork he can find and he's gonna ram it right up your fucking arse. (*Snippers pliers.*) And then, when he pulls out your kidneys on the end of his pitchfork, he's gonna flamegrill 'em and then he's gonna make you eat 'em, and if that aint enough to make you feel pretty rotten about yerself, he's gonna put his hand down your gob, right down inside your guts, and then he'll – TURN YOU INSIDE OUT! (*Demonstrates.*) Just like that. And then, if that aint enough to realise the error of your ways, he'll bring out all his little goblin friends and they'll all stand around you, and you'll be all inside out with all yer meat hanging out, and then the goblins'll start tickling yer innards with feathers, start tickling yer livers and yer lungs and it'll feel fucking strange!

ROGER nears EDDIE with the pliers. EDDIE begins to cry even more, shaking his head, begging please. He frantically tries to break free. He witters with dread and panic but not even the fear and adrenaline can help him break free. ROGER inserts the pliers slowly into EDDIE's mouth and starts to pull out a tooth. EDDIE screams as ROGER pulls it out, then ROGER pulls out another. EDDIE screams systematically. His mouth begins to fill with blood. ROGER is just about to pull out another but JANET suddenly enters. She cannot believe what she sees before her. ROGER stops his dentistry. EDDIE writhes in pain.

JANET: What the bleeding hell's going on here?

ROGER calmly sits down. He puts his feet up and lights a fag. EDDIE cries with relief. JANET isn't sure what to comprehend first: ROGER with no hair, EDDIE tied up, the stuff on the table and all of ROGER's belongings outside.

ROGER: (*Proud of the knowledge.*) Bet you didn't know Eddie's already married did yer?

JANET: (*Long pause.*) What?

ROGER: He's already married, Jan.

JANET: ... What you on about?

ROGER: (*Laughs.*) Fucker's already married to someone else.

JANET: (*Pause, not sure whether to trust him.*) How d'you know?

ROGER: (*Smiles.*) Cause I'm his son.

FADE TO BLACK.

SCENE SIX

Sometime later. Lights fade up to reveal JANET pacing up and down the room, her hand over her mouth. She is in shock. She looks at EDDIE who is still tied up in the chair, goes to scream at him, refrains, paces up and down again. Blood drips from EDDIE's mouth. He is drained and tired and in desperate need of medical attention. ROGER sits on the sofa. He mouths something to EDDIE, makes a small wanking gesture. Then he sticks out his chin, pulls his finger across his throat at EDDIE as if to say "You're dead". The urn takes pride of place in the middle of the table. JANET keeps pacing up and down, then she finally goes for it. She takes off her slipper and slippers EDDIE a good few times. A draught of foot odour lingers.

JANET: (*Screaming.*) You lying bastard! You lying bleeder!

ROGER: Go on, Jan, hit him.

JANET: You can shuddup 'en all!

EDDIE cannot speak properly because of ROGER's dental work.

EDDIE: Please... get me to a hospital.

JANET: How could yer?

EDDIE: Please... I'm gonna bleed to death!

JANET: All these years! All the years we've been together and you already had a wife and a love child!

EDDIE: He... is... not... my... bleeding love child!

JANET: I mean, how many other things have yer lied to me about?

EDDIE: I didn't lie!

JANET: No, scuse me. You lied to me. (*Thumbing herself.*) I know what lying means and I know what lying doesn't mean, sunshine.

EDDIE: But I wasn't lying, I just dint tell yer everything.

JANET: (*Pointing.*) Look in the dictionary. (*Staring at him.*) How would *you* feel if *you* came home from work and found out I had a wife and a love child?

EDDIE: For the last time – he is not my bleeding love child!

ROGER: I tell you something, Jan, he aint gonna get a father's day card off me.

JANET: Roger, will you shurrup! This is between yer dad and me.

EDDIE: Look at him, even if I knew, d'yer really think I'd tell people he was me son?

JANET: He can't help it if he's Welsh!

EDDIE: Look, it's all in the past. Please, get me to the infirmary!

ROGER: I'll get you to an infirmary in a minute, sunshine.

JANET: Roger – it's the last time I tell yer! (*Back with EDDIE.*) You told me you dint wanna get married cause you dint believe in it!

EDDIE: Please... I can explain it all.

JANET: I don't wanna hear it, I've had a gutful of your lies, you make me sick!

EDDIE: ... I'll make it up to yer!

JANET: You'll never be able to make up for what you've done, never! Cause I'll tell you something sunshine – there aint no scorn like a woman's scorn.

EDDIE: ... Paracetamol... please!

JANET: Paracetamol! I'll give you paracetamol in a minute! You deserve to go to hell!

ROGER: (*Waves fag packet in air.*) Hear hear!

JANET: Roger – if you don't shuddup, I'll hit yer with me shoe! And it's got a stiletto on it.

ROGER: (*Holds up hands.*) Sure Jan, no problem.

EDDIE: No, look, untie us, and first thing tomorrow morning, we'll go and see one of them Relate counsellors, how about that? These things always work themselves out.

JANET: There aint nought to work out, I've washed me hair wi' yer! I really have. (*To ROGER.*) I bet your mum's glad she's rid of him aint she? Hey?

ROGER: (*Nods at urn.*) Not really, no.

JANET: (*Taken aback.*) Oh. Oh dear. I'm sorry.

ROGER: Don't be. He's the one who should be sorry! Dead sorry! He goes around the corner for a bag of chips in 1974 and never comes back! Twenty-four years we waited for him to return!

JANET: Oh dear. (*Looking at urn.*) Is she? Is she in there?

ROGER: 'Fraid so. (*Takes lid off urn, looks in.*) I couldn't bear thinking about her buried beneath the soil, d'yer know what I'm saying, Jan? It's weird when I think about it, when I see her in here. She was born, met him, suffered, died, and then ended up in a vase. (*Studies the urn with pride.*) Not that this is any old vase. See that line there? Gold-plated enamel. No expenses spared.

JANET: ... How long? How long has she, yer know, been in there?

ROGER: Be about seven months now, we've travelled all over the country together, looking for him. She knows I'll never leave her on her own. (*Puts the lid back on the urn.*) God threw away the mould when he made my mam, he really did, Jan. She deserved better but the only thing she ever got from him was grief.

JANET: I can understand you feeling that way, Roger, I really can.

ROGER: I've been hurting a lot, Jan.

JANET: I'm sure you have.

ROGER: I cried myself to sleep sometimes I did. Waiting for him to turn up. Not one letter, Jan, not one, not nothing in all them years.

EDDIE: (*Wearily.*) I keep telling yer! You wunt get any letters from me cause you sodding moved house!

ROGER: He could have tried to find us, couldn't he, Jan?

JANET: (*Shaking head.*) I don't know what to say, Roger, I really don't. I can only apologise for him.

ROGER: And the worst thing about all of this is – that

bastard over there is gonna be rich now, can you believe it? He walks out on us, cheats on us and he's gonna get my mum's life assurance!

EDDIE: Really?

ROGER: Whoa whoa – I'm gonna make sure you don't see a penny of it, pal!

JANET: Damn right he shunt, 'ts disgusting how the law works.

ROGER: Disgusting! It's a fucking travesty.

EDDIE: Please, I don't want any money! Look, untie us, then I'll take yer both for a drink, then afterwards I'll throw in a Chinese. We'll have sweet and sour, special fried rice (*Excited, hoping that he's sold them the idea.*) And I'll tell yer what – just through the kindness of me heart – I'll chuck in a couple of spring rolls! (*Laughs.*) Yeah, I will (*Nodding.*) Some spring rolls!

JANET: No! You've played pass the arsehole with me for too long! Why I ever put up with it for all these years I do not know! Every day, every weekend, day in, day out watching you sitting in that chair, waiting to be taken out, waiting for you to show me some love and affection for once in yer life!

EDDIE: I can change! People change! We can still get married! We shunt let a little thing like this wreck a beautiful relationship!

JANET: You must be joking!

EDDIE: (*Desperate.*) No, I'm serious! Roger can even be best man!

ROGER: (*Claps.*) Dream on! Dream on!

EDDIE: I'll even take yer to Minehead for our honeymoon! Butlins! I will! I'll get 'em to put some red roses on the bed for yer!

JANET: (*Pause, it hurts.*) When have you ever bought me a single flower?

EDDIE goes to respond but even he knows that this is a shameful truth. JANET sits down at the table, puts her hands over her face, about to cry.

ROGER: You're no good to anybody, look at yer. You're not even any use to the dogs. If I cut you up into little pieces and left you in bags, not even the dogs would want yer. Even if I drawn, quartered and hung you, and took your bodybits in my car to the medical research people, they wunt want you either. They'd tell me to go away! They'd say I was mad! They'd look into the bag I was offering them and they'd think I was a loony! Wunt they, Jan? (*JANET nods.*) Same goes with the pigs, they wunt want you either. (*Excited by his conclusion.*) None of them want you! Not the dogs, not the pigs, not even men of the medical profession!

JANET: See, he'll listen to you, Roger.

ROGER: And listen he shall, Jan, cause I wanted to better all that by saying he's not even any use to himself.

EDDIE: ... Now you listen to me... Who d'yer think sang yer to sleep at night? Hey? Who was there for yer when yer mam had one of her turns? ... I loved yer, I cared for yer! (*ROGER stops, listens.*) I used to have yer in me arms and sing Rock-a-bye Baby to yer, I did, I was always there for yer! You used to be in tears after yer mam thought the devils were coming! I even read stories to yer at night-time!

ROGER: No you didn't.

EDDIE: I did! Yer favourite was The Owl and the Pussy Cat!

ROGER: Liar.

EDDIE: It's true!

ROGER: I don't even like cats.

EDDIE: But we even went to find yer a cat! We went into town to find yer one, went to the market, the two of us did and we bought Fluffy, a kitten, a small fluffy one. You adored it!

ROGER: Yeah – and it died.

EDDIE: ... I still paid good money for it though!

JANET quickly leaves the room, about to burst in tears.

EDDIE: ... Please, look, I've just remembered! I've even got a present for yer! I've kept it all these years!

ROGER: What present?

EDDIE: ... It's over there, in the cupboard.

ROGER looks over to the cupboard, then back at EDDIE. Then he slowly goes over to the cupboard, rummages around and brings out an old and faded wrapped present. ROGER isn't sure how to react. He doesn't trust EDDIE. He just studies the package.

EDDIE: ... I was meant to give it to yer years ago... for yer ninth birthday... It isn't the best of presents... just a little something, that's all.

ROGER looks at the present, then back at EDDIE. He un-wraps it. It is a painted wooden car. His chin starts to quiver, then his eyes start to water. Then without warning, he puts his arms around EDDIE and starts to cry. EDDIE isn't sure how to react at first but his mood lightens in winning ROGER's affections over. ROGER keeps his head on EDDIE's shoulder so that no-one can see his tears.

ROGER: I love you, I fucking love you!

EDDIE: (*Estatic.*) I love you too!

ROGER: You're my daddy!

EDDIE: (*Happy and relieved.*) That's right lad, I am. I AM!

ROGER: I fucking love you, daddy!

EDDIE: ... I love you too!

EDDIE is over the moon that they have made friends. He is like a man rescued from the claws of something awful. Tears of joy roll down his cheeks. But suddenly ROGER pulls away from him, laughing. He laughs so much he holds his crutch in fear of pissing himself. EDDIE's smile slowly disintegrates. ROGER stops laughing.

ROGER: (*To EDDIE.*) You miserable little cunt. Do you really think I'm gonna forget everything by receiving a wooden fucking car! (*Picks up pliers.*) Trying to make a mockery out of me with cheap wooden toys!

EDDIE: (*Trying another route.*) Roger, please, let's be sensible. Roger! Roger lad, 'ave yer heard that joke? (*Sheer desperation.*) What do yer call a sheep tied to a lamp post in Swansea?

ROGER: ... I don't know.

EDDIE: (*Pause.*) A leisure centre!

EDDIE gives out a feeble laugh. ROGER just stares at him, far from impressed. He launches at him and pulls out another tooth with his pliers. EDDIE screams.

ROGER: (*Gags him with a tea towel.*) Stop yer whinging man!

JANET comes back in. She has been crying and clutches some toilet roll. She sits down and tries to dry her eyes. ROGER sees this and slowly goes over to her and sits down next to her.

ROGER: Don't cry. He aint worth it, Jan.

JANET: ... All these years I was waiting to be taken up the aisle... I was gonna have a proper church wedding... organ player... all the friends from work there, it was gonna be beautiful, Roger, absolutely beautiful! And then, we were gonna go Butlins for our honeymoon... I've never been to Butlins, I've been wanting to go there all my life.

ROGER: It wasn't meant to be, that's all.

JANET: All these years we've been together. Go on God, tell me what I've got to show for it... Marriage and kids is the only thing I've ever wanted. Everytime my ship comes in, something happens to sink it.

ROGER: He doesn't have to make your life a misery anymore.

JANET: Phhh. You wanna bet?

ROGER: (*Excited.*) Well, I've been thinking – and I was wondering if I could run it past you, Jan.

JANET: What?

ROGER: Let's kill him!

EDDIE's muffles get louder, shaking his head adamantly. He rocks in his chair in an attempt to break free.

JANET: Yer what?

ROGER: (*Proud of the idea.*) Let's just kill the fucker!

JANET: Kill him? We can't just kill him.

EDDIE agrees.

ROGER: Oh yes we can. (*Clicks fingers.*) We can bump the fucker off, just like that!

JANET: You can't just kill someone.

EDDIE agrees once more.

ROGER: Well why not? He aint no use to anybody other than for taking the piss out of, is he?

JANET: ... He's yer dad.

EDDIE nods vigorously.

ROGER: More reason to kill the fucker then. Think about it, it'll be easy. How many people would know he's gone?

JANET: Knowing him, no-one.

ROGER: See.

JANET: Roger, I know he's done wrong, but it's murder. "Thou shalt not kill" – the Bible.

ROGER: Jan, if God was here with us now, even he would want to kill him. *(Gets out a document from his pocket, shows it to JANET.)* Look, we can even be rich, he doesn't deserve this money mum's left him. It was you, me and me mam who had to go without a penny all these years. My mum didn't pay all this money in just so he can get his hands on it.

JANET studies the document.

JANET: (*Mouths it.*) It's murder.

EDDIE nods in agreement.

ROGER: Look, can't you see? Eddie could be the goose that's gonna lay the golden egg for us. We're talking £50,000 here.

JANET: ... But you'll get caught, you'll go to prison.

ROGER: But we wunt get caught would we? We'd make it look like a suicide or something.

JANET: Roger, you can't kill another human being.

ROGER: Human being. That, over there, is the afterbirth.

JANET thinks about it. EDDIE squeals like a pig, shaking his head to JANET. JANET looks at EDDIE.

JANET: ... We can't.

EDDIE stops squealing and slumps into the chair with relief.

ROGER: You surprise me, Jan. I thought you had more guts.

JANET: I have got guts, I just don't agree in what yer saying.

ROGER: Fair enough. Well, I better get going. I've already caused you too much heartbreak. I'm sorry that I was the one who had to tell yer. (*Kisses her on the cheek.*) Well Jan, so long, you take good care of yerself.

ROGER gets his coat and carefully picks up the urn and goes over to the door. EDDIE suddenly feels that there may be light at the end of the tunnel until...

JANET: Don't go... Please, stay with me.

ROGER pauses. JANET starts to cry again. He puts down the urn and goes over to her. EDDIE despairs.

JANET: ... Will you hold me?

He puts his arms around her to comfort her. He gets out his hanky and tries to dry her eyes.

JANET: ... Why do I always pick the wrong man? What's wrong with me?

ROGER: Awww there's nothing wrong wi' yer.

JANET: (*Sobbing.*) Yes there is.

ROGER: You shunt be so hard on yerself gel.

JANET: ... I hate meself.

ROGER: Aww Jan, no yer don't.

JANET: I do.

ROGER: You're yer own best friend, Jan, never forget that.

JANET looks at the urn.

JANET: ... Was yer mum better looking than me? Was she slim?

ROGER: Jan – looks don't come into it. Beauty comes from within. It's a bit like the urn, it aint the urn that counts, it's what's inside that matters.(*Pondering over the urn.*) She was a bit like you, you know, she stood her ground, there was some fire in her heart.

JANET: (*Drying eyes.*) It's a very beautiful urn.

ROGER: Well it was the best I could buy, top of the range. (*Takes off lid.*) Do yer want to see?

JANET doesn't know if she wants to, but then she actually feels honoured that ROGER is showing her his mother's ashes. She peers in. ROGER has a 'impressing isn't it' look on his face.

JANET: Was she nice? Was she a nice person?

ROGER: Jan, she wouldn't be a scratch on you.

JANET: ... I bet she dint have a big bottom.

ROGER: Jan – all women get big arses at your age.

JANET bursts into tears. ROGER realises he's said the wrong thing.

ROGER: No Jan, no, I didn't mean it like that, I mean... all women, well they blossom don't they? Get more voluptuous.

JANET: No you don't, you think I've got a big bottom, everyone does.

ROGER: No I don't, you've got a lovely arse, Jan!

JANET: No I haven't.

ROGER: Yeahh you have, you've got a wonderful arse. I mean, men like something to grab onto don't they?

JANET: (*Snivels.*) I suppose so.

ROGER: See that's better – go on, let's see yer smile again, go on. (*JANET smiles.*) See, that's the Janet I know! (*Pinches her arse.*) If you ask me I think yer bleddy lovely, Jan! (*JANET is embarrassed.*) You aint getting embarrassed again are yer gel?

JANET: Well I haven't been complimented in a long time, that's why. He just says I'm fat.

ROGER: Jan – he don't know where his bread's buttered.

JANET: I mean I've tried everything. I've been on diets, Weight Watchers and all that, but it don't do no good.

ROGER: Aww Jan. You've not.

JANET: I have, I've physically starved meself at times, Roger, I have.

ROGER: God made you as you are, Jan, 'ts nothing to be ashamed of.

JANET: Yeah, well I...

ROGER: If God wanted yer thin, he would have made yer thin, wunt he?

JANET: ... I suppose so.

ROGER: (*Squeezes her thigh.*) There's nought wrong with a bit of fat now and again, is there?

JANET: I suppose not.

ROGER: You've got to put confidence back into yerself gel. Big is beautiful - don't you ever forget that.

JANET: Well, I don't wanna be big, Roger. I mean, I go into clothes shops these days and I start sweating, some of the skirts they have wunt even fit my right thigh. I get depressed I do sometimes when I look in the mirror. It's even worse when I go past the school. All the kids call me names like... Mrs Blobby.

ROGER: They're just kids, Jan, they're cruel to anyone.

JANET: ... It upsets me it does, sometimes I sit on me own and cry. Then I eat more cause I feel miserable.

ROGER: Aww Jan, Jan. I think yer lovely.

JANET: (*About to cry.*) Do yer?

ROGER: Yeahhhhh, why shunt a?

JANET: ... I don't know.

ROGER: (*Puts arm around her.*) Not all men are like that cunt over there.

JANET: (*Wipes a tear away.*) I don't deserve all these compliments.

ROGER: Rubbbbbbish! You're a lovely-looking woman. (*Pause.*) And yer sexy!

JANET: You're just taking the mickey now.

ROGER: I'm not! Turn me on yer do!

JANET: Gerrrout!

EDDIE starts to rock in his chair again, desperately trying to grab JANET's attention, wanting her not to listen to anything ROGER is saying.

ROGER: You're the woman I was supposed to always meet but never did. Stand up gel, let's see how sexy yer are!

JANET: I daren't, I'm too shy.

ROGER: Go on! Let the world see how beautiful you are!

JANET slowly and reluctantly stands up. ROGER gives her a wink that puts her at ease.

ROGER: (*Long pause.*) Why don't you go upstairs and slip into something 'more comfortable'?

JANET leans against the table, folds her arms. She isn't sure if ROGER is serious or not. ROGER winks at her. She looks over at EDDIE.

ROGER: Don't worry about him, Jan. For too long he's taken you for granted... Now he can see what he's never gonna have again.

She stares at ROGER. She comes away from him, pauses, looks back at him. Then she goes over to EDDIE, excitedly. She gives him a seductive look. EDDIE just watches her. She is enlightened by the idea of making EDDIE jealous. She exits upstairs. ROGER lights a fag, he goes over to EDDIE menacingly.

ROGER: Never been a good lover have you, Eddie? Not with me mam, not even with Jan. What is it about you? Perhaps you don't like women. Perhaps you don't like women one bit. Perhaps you prefer schoolgirls. That's what you think about isn't it? (*EDDIE shakes his head.*) Little schoolgirls in sexy underwear, little missies in short hotpants, little sexies in their sexies, is that what you think about? The fact is, I'm gonna show Jan what love is, and the difference between you and me is simple – I'm a romantic and you're a twat.

ROGER taps fag ash over EDDIE's head and then goes over to EDDIE's record collection. He finds a record he likes.

JANET comes downstairs. She stands in the hallway entrance. She wears a nightie, a pair of white high heels and has a red ribbon in her hair. She has also rouged her cheeks. She looks at ROGER, shy and seductive. ROGER looks her up and down and gives her a 'not bad, not bad' look. EDDIE just views the madness of it all. She walks past EDDIE in a way that she imagines women who are hard-to-get walk.

JANET: (*To EDDIE.*) Don't look at what yer can't afford.

ROGER gives JAN a look of 'You tell him, Jan' and then he plays the record on the stereo. It is "Can't Take My Eyes Off You" by Andy Williams. He holds out his hand to JANET.

ROGER: Would Madam care for a dance?

JANET beams with delight. ROGER goes over to her, jigging as he does so. He puts his arms around her, with a fag in one hand. JANET enjoys making EDDIE jealous. She is over-whelmed by the romance of it and feelings that have been lying dormant for many years. ROGER squeezes her arse. JANET giggles. She hasn't felt like this for such a long time. ROGER dances how he imagines a gigolo dances with rich older women in Monaco. He mimes some of the words to JANET which makes her happy but in other cases would turn women off. EDDIE looks distant and wistful as he watches them dance. The song finishes. JANET and ROGER look at each other. They realise that even the ugly need love. They begin to kiss. ROGER feels like Valentino, JANET just feels wanted. EDDIE begins to sob. He can't bare to watch them any longer. They stop kissing. ROGER whispers something into her ear. JANET giggles. He takes her by the hand and leads her to the bottom of the stairs. But just before they go upstairs, JANET turns to EDDIE.

JANET: Your son knows how to treat a woman. (*Pause.*) And – I bet he lasts longer than five seconds.

They both disappear up the stairs excitedly. EDDIE's head drops to the floor, his back goes up and down as he cries.

BLACKOUT.

SCENE SEVEN

"Songs of Praise" is on television. JANET sits on the sofa happily painting her toenails in her nightgown.

EDDIE is still gagged and bound to the chair. ROGER has put the wig on EDDIE's head. He looks the worse for wear, almost broken. ROGER sits at the table wearing a vest, underpants and socks. They have 'dynamite' written around the front bit. He still wears his tinted glasses. He looks pissed off with his arms folded.

JANET: (*Thinks.*) Cushion.

ROGER: Not even warm.

JANET: Well what is it then?

ROGER: What?

JANET: What is it?

ROGER: Jan, what's the point in playing I spy when I tell you what it is.

JANET: Well I won't know what it is else will a?

ROGER: Jan, I'm not being blunt or anything, but that's part of the game.

JANET: Oh. (*Pause, looks around the room.*) I spy with my little eye something beginning with F.

ROGER: (*Just staring at her.*) What?

JANET: I spy with my little eye something beginning with F.

ROGER: (*Just staring at her.*) No Jan, you've got to guess what mine is first.

JANET: Oh.

ROGER: Well go on then.

JANET: I'm trying to think. (*As if she's caught ROGER out.*) Ahhhh, ahhhhhh but how do I know you won't lie, so I could say cushion, and you could say it isn't.

ROGER: Trust me, Jan, trust me.

JANET: (*Thinks.*) Well cushion's the only thing I can think of.

ROGER puts his hands over his face.

JANET: We could play charades. I'm good at that.

ROGER: Forget it, Jan, just forget it.

JANET: Well what was it?

ROGER: Just leave it, Jan.

JANET: Go on, what was it?

ROGER: (*Pointing at EDDIE.*) CUNT! ALRIGHT? CUNT! CUNT! CUNT!

JANET: (*Upset.*) There's no need to shout, I was only asking.

ROGER: I'm sorry, alright? I'm sorry, I didn't mean to shout.

JANET sulks. ROGER goes over to her. He sits down next to her, gives her a reassuring hug. JANET smiles. She continues painting her nails. ROGER goes to say something but JANET interrupts.

JANET: Roger, yer not killing yer dad.

ROGER huffs. He looks at the ceiling and the walls, lets out a big sigh.

ROGER: Well, what we gonna do with him then?

JANET: We'll think of something, that's all I know.

ROGER: Yeah, and what then?

JANET: Well, he'll leave, make someone else's life a misery.

ROGER: No he won't, he'll go straight to the police and tell 'em about my dental work.

JANET: Roger – yer not killing yer dad. (*She holds out her hands in front of ROGER.*) D'yer like me nail varnish? I've put it on especially for you, it's Moonlight Blue. (*Pinches him.*) Cause you said I was the stars. Go on, say it again, say what yer said to me, say what yer said to me upstairs.

ROGER: ... You're my moon, my stars, my sun... and my black hole.

JANET: Ahhh, that's lovely. Thank you for what happened upstairs. Aint felt like that for a long time. You know what to do wi' yer hands don't yer?

ROGER: Jan, always a pleasure, never a chore.

ROGER sniffs his fingers, pulls a face of disgust. He looks at EDDIE, and like a child who can't get his own way, points at JANET and makes a fucking gesture. JANET finishes off painting her nails. ROGER sees a Butlins brochure on the floor, next to the sofa. He picks it up, puts it back down. His brain can be seen trying to process various bits of information.

ROGER: Jan? How about us two go away together?

JANET: (*Excited.*) Really? Where?

ROGER: (*Holds up Butlins magazine.*) Hi-di-Hi, Ho-di-Ho, Jan.

JANET: Yer joking!

ROGER: No, straight off, blue.

JANET: God I'd love to!

ROGER: Same here, I aint a bleddy holiday in years! And you certainly deserve one!

JANET: (*Looks at EDDIE.*) Tell me about it!

ROGER: Just us two in a chalet together. (*As if ONASSIS.*) Full board an all.

JANET: Full board? Really?

ROGER: Well yer don't want be pissing around catering for yerself, Jan. And – I'm gonna ask 'em if we can have the honeymoon suite.

JANET: No, yer joking.

ROGER: And I'm gonna get 'em to put 100 red roses on the bed for yer!

JANET: Aww, it's like a dream this, will yer pinch me, Roger. (*ROGER pinches her. She holds her heart.*) Aww I'm having palpitations I'm so excited.

ROGER: You stick wi' me gel and I'll show you a good time. It's gonna be fucking marvellous - bingo in the evenings, a cabaret in the afternoon, they have all them people off Stars for Eyes on stage. Go-karts an all! I'll have a bang on that, blue.

JANET: I'm sure you will, car-mad you.

ROGER: (*Looking at brochure.*) Snooker and poolhall as well – I'm a wizard on the green baize, Jan.

JANET: Well you'll certainly beat me at it! Oh it's gonna be wonderful.

ROGER: Wonderful? It's gonna be smashing, blue. Tell yer what, depending what mood I'm in (*Winks.*) we could make love in the outdoor swimming pool.

JANET: (*Excited, nudges him.*) Saucy!

ROGER: Hey, look, they've got a funfair as well, Jan – the dodgems, those elephant rides that go in the air, and hey! How about this – the Tunnel of Love.

JANET: Aww how beautiful.

ROGER: And yer know what happens if a woman comes into the Tunnel of Love with me?

JANET: (*Smiling.*) What?

ROGER: You go in a lady, come out a whore.

JANET: I'm sure you do! God, I shall have to buy some new holiday clothes!

ROGER: Treat yerself, blue.

JANET: I shall have to have me hair done too, I've always fancied one of them Leisure perms.

ROGER: Go for it!

JANET: God, the girls at work are gonna be so jealous of me! When are we going then?

ROGER: As soon as we get me mum's life assurance.

JANET: (*Disappointed.*) But Roger, I keep telling yer, we can't just...

ROGER: (*Interrupts.*) When was the last time he took you on holiday?

JANET: (*Thinks, ashamed to say.*)... Twenty years ago.

ROGER: See.

JANET: Yeah, but...

ROGER: Look, he hasn't taken you on holiday for 20 years! So now you can have a holiday on him can't yer?

JANET: But you can't just...

ROGER: (*Interrupts.*) Think about it, us two in Skeggy, it'll be fucking brilliant!

JANET: Skeggy? I don't want to go to the Skeggy one, I want to go to the Bognor one.

ROGER: I aint driving all the way to Bognor, Skeggy's nearer.

JANET: But Joyce's been to the Bognor one. She says it's ever so good.

ROGER: I'm sorry Jan, but Skeggy's my final offer. It makes more sense.

JANET: (*Showing him page in brochure.*) But there's more things in Bognor. Look, they've got them people dressed up as animals. 'Be greeted by Chunky the monkey – and then take a ride in the cheeky chimp's car round the complex. And look, they've got one of them indoor

water plumes as well, "The Master Blaster". (*Reads it.*)
'This death-defying water experience for couples drops
you 20 feet from the starting point, then blasts you back
up to the top for a mind-blowing 100 foot rollercoaster
ride to the finish'.

ROGER: (*Pause, computing her weight.*) I don't think that's
very wise, do you?

JANET: Are you trying to say I'm too fat for it, cause...

ROGER: Jan, I'm not saying anything, but I am not gonna
drive 300 miles south just so that I can be blasted 200
foot in the air and be driven around the complex by
a monkey.

JANET: (*Considers it.*) If it's what you want.

ROGER: It is, Jan.

JANET: (*Looking over at EDDIE.*)... So if I did agree to, yer
know, killing him, how would you do it?

ROGER: (*Claps hands.*) We'll think of something, blue!

BLACKOUT

SCENE EIGHT

*Fade up with the sound of choking and coughing to reveal
EDDIE tied to the table. He is surrounded by various bottles
of tablets, lotions and cleaning liquids. JANET stands over
him, emptying various bottles of tablets down his throat. He
looks ill and sick with all the tablets that he has swallowed.
ROGER sits on the sofa, writing out a suicide note.*

EDDIE: ... I'll give yer the money! Money aint important to
me... oh God, oh please... Please don't do this to me...

Janet! Please! You'll never know how much I love yer!
... cause I do! I know I never deserved yer! You'd kill me
if you ever left me... You were always too good for me,
you put up with more than you should 'ave done, but
I can change, we can turn back the clock... Remember
when we went to Blackpool for the weekend? We can
do all that again, we can go next week, no, we can go
tomorrow...

JANET: (*Arms folded.*) Roger's taking me to Skeggy.

EDDIE: Well, I'll take yer to Skeggy!

JANET: Well Roger's paying for a honeymoon suite.

EDDIE: ... I'll pay for a week in the honeymoon suite too!

ROGER: Ahhhh but I'm taking her for two weeks!

EDDIE: Then I'll take her for three weeks!

ROGER: Then I'll take her for a month!

JANET: Hear that? Roger's taking me for a whole month!

*JANET empties some more tablets down his throat and, to
help EDDIE wash them down, she pours some Domestos down
his throat. EDDIE tries to move his head but he is too weak.
He groans and his mouth froths up with fluid.*

JANET: Roger – shall I give him some Toilet Duck as well?

ROGER: Yeah, throw it in, blue.

*JANET picks up the Toilet Duck, tears off a "20p off next
purchase" voucher and squirts it into EDDIE's mouth. Then
she gags him with a tea towel so that he can't spit the tablets
back out. EDDIE groans.*

JANET: It will be alright, won't it?

ROGER: Trust me, Jan, trust me.

JANET: He won't come back and haunt us will he?

ROGER: Jan – he doesn't know his arse from his elbow, leave alone navigating heaven and earth. Besides, he aint going to heaven, he'd stink the angels' wings up.

EDDIE vomits up the Domestos. As he pukes, his booted feet turn inwards at the pain and poorliness.

JANET: D'yer reckon I've gave him enough?

ROGER: What you gave him?

JANET: I've given him 20 sleeping tablets, about thirty pain killers for his arthritis, some paracodeine, (*Reading bottle.*) 40 Phyllocontin – 250 milligram, some vitamin pills...

ROGER: Jan – we supposed to be killing the fucker, not give him a sense of well being.

JANET: Well I didn't know.

ROGER: Go on, what else?

JANET: ... Some Toilet Ducky, 60, no, hold on, no, 50 salbutomol tablets, a drop of Windowlene, I couldn't use all of it, Roger cause I've got to do me kitchen windows tomorrow, and some Diocalm.

ROGER: Diocalm? He aint got diarrhoea, Jan.

JANET: That's all I could find.

ROGER: He aint gonna die on Diocalm.

JANET: Well I dint know did a?

ROGER: Right, well the sleeping tablets should do the trick. What d'yer reckon to this? (*Reads out.*) "Dear God, dear baby Jesus, I can stand this life no more, it is such a horrible world out there and I want nothing more to do with it... I hope heaven can show me the kindness I deserve in life... I leave all my possessions and foregoing moneys to Janet, and my loving son, Roger... Goodbye, yours faithfully... Eddie... kiss kiss."

JANET: That sounds good, Roger. You could write poetry you could.

ROGER: No flies round me, Jan.

JANET: So what do we do now?

ROGER: Sit and wait, fucker'll be dead in no time.

FADE OUT.

Fade up. Sometime later. JANET is hoovering the carpet. ROGER is just staring at EDDIE, bemused. Then, ROGER sees that EDDIE is still and silent. ROGER gets up, slowly goes over to him, he stands over EDDIE in excited anticipation that he is finally dead. ROGER pokes him. EDDIE jerks suddenly and starts to groan again. ROGER puts his hands over his face in despair.

FADE OUT.

FADE UP.

SCENE NINE

ROGER paces up and down the room waiting for EDDIE to die. He looks pissed off. EDDIE's feet twitch and he has a slight spasm in his index finger as various chemicals attack his body. JANET reads the Argos catalogue. Then she sees ROGER'S mood, and pats the space on the sofa next to her.

JANET: Come and sit yerself down Rog, be patient.

ROGER: I'm a little bit tense at the moment, Jan.

JANET lifts up her arm and looks at ROGER seductively.

JANET: I've shaved me armpits for yer, Rog, come and have a feel.

ROGER: Yer what?

JANET: I said I've shaved me armpits. I know yer don't like bodily hair.

ROGER: (*Preoccupied.*) Yeah, lovely.

JANET: Well look then.

ROGER: I'm looking!

JANET: Don't have to shout at me.

ROGER: Jan, I'm waiting for me dad to die, alright?

JANET: Well come and sit on the sofa then, feel me armpits, soft as silk they are.

ROGER: Jan, please.

JANET: Don't you love me anymore?

ROGER: Yes!

JANET: Well if you loved me, you'd look at me armpits.

ROGER rolls his eyes back, looks at her armpit.

ROGER: I'm looking, look.

JANET: Not like that. You should do it with more seduction.

ROGER: Jan, please.

ROGER continues to pace up and down the room. Silence, then...

JANET: I shunt have to ask yer to look at me armpits, you should want to look at 'em.

ROGER: Jan, when me dad's dead, I can look at yer armpits all the while, alright?

ROGER looks out into the street, pissed off, impatient.

JANET: Look, perhaps there's other ways of killing him.

ROGER: Like what, Jan?

JANET: Well, yer know, we could do what these murderers do, they chop the person's head off and then bury the body in a field somewhere else.

ROGER: I think we're on a different frequency here. The whole reason we're making it look like a suicide is so that people can see it's a suicide.

JANET: ... So?

ROGER: So it's gonna look a bit odd when the man from the Prudential comes round and sees Eddie sitting in a corn field with no fucking head!

FADE OUT.

FADE UP.

ROGER is sitting on the sofa smoking a fag. JANET stands in front of him touching her nose and pointing, then pretending her hand is a camera. ROGER just watches on, bored and disinterested as JANET plays charades to kill time. She has learnt all the manoeuvres from Lionel Blair. EDDIE froths at the mouth, he keeps drifting in and out of consciousness.

FADE OUT.

SCENE TEN

ROGER polishes his mother's urn. EDDIE has become more animated in his twitching and groaning. JANET sees this, she goes over to him concerned. EDDIE keeps moving his fingers and the muffled sound of him asking for JANET can be heard. There is a sense of urgency about him. JANET removes his gag and beckons ROGER over. They stand over him. EDDIE tries to speak, mustering up every last breath he has.

JANET: I think he wants to say his last wish, Roger... (*To EDDIE.*) What is it luv?... What is it?... Is it yer last wish?... A what?... want a what?... A satsuma? (*EDDIE gives a weak nod.*) ... He wants a satsuma, Roger... Will yer go and get him one?

ROGER: I'm not getting him a satsuma, after what he's done.

JANET: Roger, I know he's done wrong, but he's still yer dad. Go and fetch him a satsuma...

ROGER reluctantly goes off to the kitchen. He brings out a satsuma. JANET peels it. Eddie's tied hands twitch, grasping and clutching thin air for the satsuma. JANET tries to peel it as fast as she can, reassuring him that it's coming. EDDIE's mouth opens and closes in desperation and his feet make small kicks. But just as JANET has finished peeling the orange, EDDIE goes still and silent and his head hangs to one side. His feet twitch just one more time and then nothing. JANET and ROGER look at each other. There is a stony silence, then ROGER listens to EDDIE's heart. He looks at JANET, who feels both a sadness and the anticipation of EDDIE's finality. ROGER looks at JANET, then he gives her the thumbs up. There is a short moment and then they hug in the celebration of their victory.

JANET: Shall I make some celebratory sandwiches?

ROGER: Good idea, Jan.

JANET: What would yer like?

ROGER: (*Winks.*) Surprise me, Jan, surprise me.

JANET goes into the kitchen excitedly to make the sandwiches. ROGER stands over EDDIE's body, lights a fag. He listens to JANET singing happily in the kitchen. He is not excited, then he goes over to the urn, he holds it, hugs it. It's almost as if his mother died the very minute EDDIE did. He gives the urn a kiss, as if the lid is his mother's lips. He rests his head against it and cradles it with love. It is a quiet and private moment. He puts the vase back down carefully and as if holding his mother's hand for the last time, strokes it gently.

ROGER: (*Whispering.*) Goodbye mother. It's over now. "I love you more today than yesterday but less than tomorrow."

JANET comes in with a plate of sandwiches. She places them on the table and sits down. She is like a new woman, radiating energy and vitality. ROGER just watches her.

JANET: Come and have yer sandwiches luv.

ROGER sits down opposite her at the table. EDDIE's lifeless body between them. JANET eats joyfully with the occasional 'uhmm, uhmm'. ROGER looks at his sandwich. There is a definite change about him. He carries the same menace as he did alone with EDDIE. JANET gets out a bikini. She holds it in the air proudly. ROGER just stares at her with disinterest and no emotion. JANET is oblivious.

JANET: (*Sings.*) "She was afraid to come out of the water, So she wore an itsy bitsy teeny weeny yellow polkadot bikini!"

Silence. ROGER just stares at her twiddling with his moustache. JANET's smiling disperses. She is aware of

ROGER's sudden change of personality. She puts the bikini down. JANET ignores his stare and eats her sandwich.

ROGER: (*Calm and slow.*) This sandwich smells and looks like shit.

JANET: Pardon?

ROGER: (*Staring at her.*) I said this sandwich looks and smells like crap.

JANET: (*Taken aback, slightly scared.*) What's wrong with it?

ROGER: (*Slow and threatening.*) What did I say to yer?

JANET: ... What?

ROGER: I said I wanted a surprise. What's so fucking surprising about a slice of cheese? You'd be good at the Kinder Surprise factory wunt yer? Hey? The kid'd look inside the egg and all he'd find is a lump of fucking cheese!

JANET: It's food isn't it? I thought you liked cheese.

ROGER: Don't give me that "It's food int it" bollocks! It smells and looks like shit. Like everything else you make!

JANET: I'm sorry, that's all I could find.

ROGER: You're gonna be sorry in a minute. Dead sorry. (*ROGER looks in the sandwich again.*) You'd be good in a restaurant wunt yer? Hey? Boss'd ask you to come up with some new flavours, and you'd come up with cheese. Cheese and cheese. Cheese on cheese, cheese filling. (*Pauses, thinks of more cheese variations.*) Cheese with cheese. Cheese with extra cheese. Choose yer own cheese. Cheese buffet. Cheese extra. You've got no imagination whatsoever have yer? Got none at all. No wonder all your food's crap and I had to eat those terrible fucking tomato sauce sandwiches. That's why you're a cleaner, cause no-one else will employ yer, the creative side of yer brain's gone cold, looks like a jellied eel. They wunt have you in a sandwich stall either. Cause first of all, you'd scare all the customers away. Secondly, no-one would want your fat stinky fingers on their sarnies, and thirdly – as I've said before – you haven't got any imagination. They'd just be cheese right across the board. Cheese this, cheese that, cheese madam, cheese can I have some more sir! (*Throws sandwiches at her. JANET is in a quiet shock.*) Who do you think I am? Do you really think I'm stupid enough to go "Oh yeah, great, nice sandwich Janet" and sits back and eat it? (*Throws plate at wall.*) Now get back in the kitchen and make me another sandwich and if I find one speck of fucking cheese, so God help me you're gonna wish cheese was never invented!

JANET slowly gets up. She isn't sure what to say or do. She gingerly heads for the kitchen. As she goes by, ROGER picks up the sandwich, throws it at the back of JANET's head. ROGER sits back down, breathing heavily through his nose. JANET goes into the kitchen. She makes another sandwich. She looks at ROGER with both concern and fear. She comes back in, places the sandwich in front of ROGER. She sits down and waits for ROGER's response. Roger looks in the sandwich, sniffs it, sniffs it again, looks at JANET, then sniffs it once more for good measure. He begins to eat it. JANET watches him. She peps up a little, smiles.

JANET: ... I can't wait till we go... It's gonna be wonderful. (*ROGER ignores her.*) I can see us now, putting our cases in your car... you checking the oil... me making some special sandwiches for our journey... and then we'll set off at the crack of dawn... (*ROGER just eats.*) The sun'll just be coming up ... and we'll be driving, driving away from this house and all the rotten memories... and then soon we'll be in the countryside... and then we'll find a little lay-by and have our pickernic... then we'll be off again... the windows open... and then the bottom of the sky will get bluer and bluer and we'll know the sea is just at the bottom of that sky... (*ROGER finishes his sandwich.*) D'yer know who we have to ring to get yer mum's money?... You know?... Who we have to ring?

ROGER: (*Long pause.*) What money?

JANET: ... Yer mum's life assurance.

ROGER: She never had any life assurance.

JANET: ... Yes she did... You showed me the papers.

ROGER: I think you'll find they were for my car insurance.

JANET is speechless. ROGER puts on his coat, gets out his car keys.

JANET: (*Confused.*) What yer doing? Where yer going?

ROGER: Going home.

JANET: What?

ROGER: (*Smiles.*) No point in me hanging round here, I've done what I came to do.

JANET: ... I don't understand, what...

ROGER: Now give me the locket back.

JANET: (*Confused.*) What?

ROGER: Give me it back, it's not yours. It's my mum's.

JANET is not sure what to comprehend first. She gives him the locket.

ROGER: You could never replace my mum.

JANET: But what... What about...

ROGER: Always were a greedy bitch, weren't you, Jan?

JANET: ... I dunno what you mean.

ROGER: You stole my dad. You took him away from me and me mam, you took everything away.

JANET: I didn't know! He didn't tell me! It wasn't my fault!

ROGER: My mam died with a broken heart because of what you two did.

JANET tries to untie EDDIE in s desperate attempt to revive him.

ROGER: (*Tuts.*) Too late now, Jan. What's it like to murder yer own fiancé? What's it like?

JANET: You helped me! You told me to do it!

ROGER: You were the one who poured tablets down his neck.

JANET: But you helped me, you wrote the suicide note!

ROGER: (*Looks around the room.*) What suicide note?

JANET: You bastard!

ROGER: Just like me dad then aren't a? What's it like to be a murderer, Jan?

JANET: It was all your idea, you were the one who made me!

ROGER: Whatever you say, Jan, whatever.

JANET: I'll tell the police everything!

ROGER: It's your finger marks on the tablet bottles.

JANET: (*Still in shock.*) But... we were, we were gonna go on holiday, we were gonna do things together, you even told me you loved me!

ROGER: Take a look at yerself, Jan. In fact, I even feel sorry for me dad now, to think he left my mum for someone like you, me mam'd always thought he'd found a dolly bird or something, a real stunner, but I reckon my mam'd be laughing in her grave if she saw you, well, laughing in her urn if she saw you. My mam pisses all over you, Jan.

JANET starts to cry.

JANET: He didn't tell me he was married, I didn't know!

ROGER: It don't matter. You wanned to step into my mam's shoes and steal her husband away, that's what you wanted to do! (*Gets the urn, unscrews the lid.*) My mum always wanted to meet you, see what yer were like, she can meet yer now!

ROGER pours the ash over JANET. JANET screams, tries to pull him away, it goes into her hair and over her clothes. Some of it goes over ROGER's glasses and in his moustache. Then, there is nothing left. He puts the urn in JANET's arms and watches her cry. Then he heads slowly for the door. He takes one last look at EDDIE, the room, and JANET. He exits the flat and closes the door behind him. JANET looks at EDDIE's lifeless body and at the urn. ROGER's car is heard starting up, then it pulls away followed by the sound of ROGER's novelty car horn. It roars away. JANET listens as it gets fainter and fainter until it is heard no more.

FADE TO BLACK.